Succeeding:
OVERCOMING THE ODDS

PRESTWICK HOUSE, INC.

"Everything for the English Classroom!"

P.O. Box 658 • Clayton, DE 19938
Tel: 1.800.932.4593
Web site: www.prestwickhouse.com

ISBN-10: 1-58049-309-2
ISBN-13: 978-1-58049-309-3

Table Of Contents

Who Is A Success?

In this book, we have profiled a variety of people we thought were successful and whose stories were interesting. A few of these people have become well known, but most of them have not; some have become very rich, but others have not. While all of them started with very little in the way of material things, some of them came from warm, supportive families; others of them did not. All of them, however, did have to overcome obstacles to achieve their goals.

List the names of 5 people whom you consider successful. State why you think they are successes at what they do.

1.

2.

3.

4.

5.

What Price Will You Pay For Success?

In the world today, success is often measured by how much money a person has or how famous he or she is. Many people think of money and fame as the number one goal. Should money and fame be your number one goal in life? Before you respond to this, answer the following question.

Question:
A fairy godmother offered you a million dollars and said, "If you accept the money, you will be wealthy for the rest of your life, but you will endure a life filled with pain and unhappiness." What would you tell her?

Response: (State a reason for your answer.)
Since most people value happiness and freedom from pain more highly than anything else, no rational person would accept such an offer. Yet, by their everyday actions, there are people who do make that choice. In one paper, for example, was the story of a man in Chicago, a millionaire, who was sentenced to thirty-five to fifty years for dealing in drugs and conspiracy to commit murder. To be deprived of one's freedom, even for a short time, is a high price to pay for wealth.

In contrast, a life of poverty can limit a person's freedom. The hunger, drudgery, and despair that may accompany poverty can bring both pain and unhappiness.

1. Is there anyone in the news who has money or fame but appears to be unhappy?

2. Is there anyone who appears to you to have both money and happiness?

Wishes and Dreams

Most people wish for happiness and enough money for them and their families to live comfortable lives; this is a reasonable dream. Consider what your dreams are.

Write down the things you would like to have in ten years. To help you out, we have put down some broad categories, but you need not give equal attention to all of them. Do try, however, to be as specific and concrete as possible. For example, try to visualize a house and describe it, rather then just saying "a big house." Also try to identify a job or type of job, rather than just saying, "a good job."

In Ten Years...

1. What kind of education would you like to have?

2. What kind of job or career?

3. What kind of family would you like to have/create?

4. In what kind of residence would you like to be living?

5. What kind of relationships would you like to have with your parents, your friends, your husband or wife, and your own children?

6. In what hobbies or sports would you like to be involved?

7. How much money would you like to be earning?

The Difference Between Dreams and Goals

Did you ever meet people who said that their dream was to be a great musician and make a living playing in a band? Yet, when asked, they tell you they spend very little time practicing the instrument. Do you know people who say that their dream is to win a tennis or wrestling scholarship, but they put forth only the minimum effort required by the coach? For these people, their dreams will never be anything more than dreams. It is having goals, not dreams, that get things done.

Dreams are things we sit back and fantasize about, while goals are things that get us out of the chair and working toward something. Look at your list of dreams again. If you really want those things, you will turn them into goals and work for them. One writer said, "Anything that the mind can visualize, the body can bring about." We can agree with this statement, with one exception: A lack of talent, or not enough talent, may limit a person's dreams. Aside from that exception, however, we can accomplish nearly anything we would like to do.

A Five Point Program for Setting Goals

Point #1 - Identifying long-range goals.

Look back at your dream list. Identify no more than two or three dreams that are really important to you. If, for example, one of your dreams was to be involved in a relationship with a kind, sensitive person, you might have written this: "I want to be involved with a kind, sensitive person." Now, turn this "wish" statement into a "goal" statement. "In 10 years, if I am in a relationship, it will be with a kind and sensitive person." Your long-range goals, however, must be big and worthwhile because it is only this type of goal that motivates us.

Point #2 - Identify the obstacles you must overcome.

Once you identify your long-range goals, you must then determine the steps you will have to climb to reach these goals. For someone whose career goal is to become a lawyer, for example, the steps might look like this:

Become a lawyer

Graduate from law school

Graduate from college

Be accepted to college

Pass 12th grade

Pass 11th grade

Pass 10th grade

Pass 9th grade

While there may be fewer steps for the career you have chosen as your goal, everyone's short-term goal must be to graduate from high school. To accomplish that goal, however, you must first pass this year. But to pass this year, you must first pass each one of the courses you are taking. These you should view as your immediate objectives.

Point #3 - Set deadlines for your goals.

The person who just says, "Someday, I will take a trip to Europe" will probably never get there. But the person who says, "Before August 1, 2005, I am going to go to Europe," very probably will get there. He will get there simply because he planned and worked toward that end, while the first person only dreamed about doing it.

Point #4 - Develop an action plan.

In developing an action plan, it is all right to be general for ten years away. As you get closer to the present, however, try to be as specific as possible.

Diane, a senior in a vocational program, has the goal "to own her own beauty parlor." Her plan calls for her to work for someone else for seven to eight years so she can save enough money and learn the business. Therefore, it is necessary that her goal is general at this point. Her immediate goals, however, are to graduate from school, get state certification, and find a job in a *good* beauty shop where she can learn a great deal about running a shop and save some money. Notice how specific she needs to be when creating these immediate goals.

Point #5 - What's in it for me?

It is extremely important that you list what you expect to get from accomplishing your goals. The more concrete the reward, the better you can visualize it. The better you visualize the reward, the harder you will work to achieve it.

One motivational speaker urges his students to visualize the payoff as concretely as possible. If, for example, your goal is to be a successful, well-paid mechanic, you might visualize completing the work on an engine, and the customer counting out the money and paying you for the job.

Goals Are Achieved a Day or a Pound or an Inch at a Time

An actor who made it big in a movie was on a talk show last month. A woman in the audience stood up and asked him how it felt to be an overnight success. The actor explained that it took him seventeen years to be "an overnight success." He pointed out that few people know that he had gone to hundreds of auditions, waited tables for years, washed out countless garbage cans, and sometimes had nothing to eat but ketchup sandwiches. In effect, he was telling her that he may be at the top of the hill now, but it took seventeen years of working, studying, and learning his craft to get there.

A number of studies confirm that this same principle applies to losing weight and keeping it off. If your goal is to lose twenty-six pounds in a year, you can't wait until the eleventh month before you begin a program of exercise and calorie cutting. Rather, a better strategy is for you to begin immediately and lose 1/2 pound per week.

This also applies to getting a passing grade in a subject. We all know students who say in September and October, "The weather is so nice, it's too early to start working." Then they find one reason or another to continue postponing their work. In the last month of school, these students become either optimists or pessimists. The pessimist says, "It's too late now; I'll just have to fail the course." The optimist says, "I'll work hard and pass this course yet." Of course, both of them fail for the year. The realists, those who began to work the very first day and worked each and every day thereafter, were the ones who passed the course.

1. Since the start of this school year, how many days have you worked on passing this course?

2. Could you have done more?

3. If so, why didn't you do more?

Why Bother With Goals?

On a very practical level, goals get us to take action, and they keep us at the job when the going gets tough. Many people, for example, work at a second job. They don't particularly like doing this, but they do it so they can save enough money to put a down payment on a home.

Jack, an office worker during the day, worked nights on a loading dock. From six to ten, warm nights or cold, Jack loaded trucks. On some dark, winter nights, Jack was cold, hungry, and tired. Only the thought of "his house" kept him at the job. In short, a person with a realizable goal gets things done that a person without a goal does not.

More important, goals give us a purpose and direction in our lives. They also allow us to keep minor setbacks in perspective. Anna, a seventeen-year-old whose goals were to become a fashion designer and have a relationship with a kind, attractive man, was "dumped" by her boyfriend. This made her unhappy, but not *very* unhappy. With her eye on her goals, she knew that she still would be a designer and she still would have a relationship with a kind, attractive man. It just wasn't going to be with the one she had been dating.

Changing Directions

Change is an inescapable part of life. As a result, it is quite possible that you may change some of your goals, but to paraphrase the old saying, "It is better to have worked toward a goal and have changed it, than to never have had any goal at all." Whatever you have learned or accomplished in working toward that goal, you certainly will always be able to use in working toward a new goal. Daniel Inouye's goal was to become a surgeon. After he lost an arm in the war, however, he knew he had to find a new goal. Switching to law school and politics, though, was not difficult for him. The habits and attitudes he had developed earlier, he easily put to use in his new action plan.

Attitude

The tennis star Billie Jean King says that she knows which of her opponents will miss their serve. "When they stand at the line, ready to serve, you can see it in their face. They have, in their mind, pictured themselves hitting the ball into the net, and that is exactly what they do. When I stand at the line to serve, I picture myself hitting the ball squarely into their court. That is where it usually goes."

If you want to succeed at something, picture yourself doing it successfully. The student who wishes to get better grades needs to visualize doing the work and getting papers back with 90s and 100s.

Succeeding:
OVERCOMING THE ODDS

> " *I'm really paying homage to people I love, the people thought to be dumb and backward but who were the ones who first taught me to see beauty.* "

POETIC VISION

ALICE WALKER

ALICE WALKER WAS the youngest of eight children. Her father, a sharecropper, earned barely enough to keep the family alive, so her mother helped support the family by working as a maid. Of her father, Walker said, "He was wonderful at math but a terrible farmer." Although she loved both parents, she was most deeply influenced by her mother. She said, "I grew up believing there was nothing my mother couldn't do once she set her mind to it."

From her parents, she inherited her love of stories and storytelling. At the age of eight, she began to write down the stories that she had heard. From that beginning, she went on to write stories and poems of her own. Living in three rooms with ten people, however, made it difficult for her to find a place to concentrate. For this reason, she spent a lot of time outdoors thinking and writing.

Alice suffered a major setback shortly after she turned eight when her brother accidentally shot her in the eye with a BB gun. Because they had no car, her parents could not get her to the hospital for treatment until a week had passed. When the doctor finally did see her, it was too late. Alice was blind in that eye. To make matters even worse, a layer of scar tissue had formed over the eye. The child who had been happy and outgoing, now became painfully self-conscious and shy.

Teased by the other children because of her eye, Alice began to feel like an outcast. Withdrawing from the company of people, Alice turned to her reading and writing for comfort. Six years later, the scar tissue was removed. Alice re-entered a social life with her friends in high school. She said, "It allowed me to really see people and things; to really notice relationships and to learn to be patient enough to care about how they turned out." Despite her period of isolation, when Alice did return to high school, she was very popular. At graduation, she was the valedictorian of the class. She also was voted queen of the senior class by the other students. Upon her graduation, she won a scholarship to Spelman College in Atlanta. For Alice to get to the school, however, her neighbors had to raise $75.00 for the bus fare to Atlanta.

One year later, Alice transferred to Sarah Lawrence College in New York on a scholarship. When she arrived there in September, she was in a deep state of depression. Once again, she turned to her writing for comfort. During the year, she showed some of her poems to one of her teachers who was a published poet. The teacher showed the poems to a publisher, who accepted them for publication.

After graduating from college, Alice became a social activist working in Mississippi for Civil Rights. She continued writing and publishing poems and stories, but it was not until publication of her third novel, *The Color Purple*, that she became widely known. Once, when asked why she writes about poor, black people living in the backwaters of the South, she responded, "I'm really paying homage to people I love, the people thought to be dumb and backward but who were the ones who first taught me to see beauty."

Called a "womanist," a term she coined to describe black feminists, she is sometimes accused of presenting black men in her writings too negatively. To this charge she responds, "The black woman is one of America's greatest heroes. The cruelty of the black man to his wife and family is one of the great tragedies. It has mutilated the spirit and body of the black family and of most black mothers."

Comprehension Questions

1. From the context, what would you infer these words mean:

   A. backwater -

   B. Black feminist -

2. What does the expression, "When life hands you a lemon, make lemonade" mean? How does this expression apply to Ms. Walker?

3. Why does Ms. Walker consider the black woman one of America's greatest heroes?

4. What do you suppose Alice's dream was as a child?

5. What enabled her to achieve this dream?

6. In your own words, explain the significance of the title.

Succeeding:
OVERCOMING THE ODDS

" There are no
shortcuts to success.
You need an
education and you
need to work hard. "

ACADEMIC DESIRE

ANNA LANGFORD

ANNA LANGFORD HAD nothing going for her. Her grandmother lived in poverty, her mother lived in poverty, and Anna grew up in poverty. Her father, who was black, died when she was nine months old. Her mother, who was white, had no skills or resources with which to support Anna and her two sisters. The whites discriminated against Anna because her father was black, and she was discriminated against by the blacks because her mother was white. Worst of all, she felt discriminated against by both groups because she was poor.

Her mother, who had remarried, died when Anna was nine. As a result, Anna and her sisters were sent to live with her grandmother. Her grandmother lived in a tarpaper shack with her own two sisters. One of the grandmother's sisters was too ill to work. The other was an alcoholic who would not work. Anna recalled, "Grandmother worked for five different families as a domestic, twelve hours a day, six days a week. Two things stand out most vividly in my mind about those terrible days," she said. "In winter we were always cold, and all year long we were almost always hungry. I vowed to myself that when I got older, I would never be cold and hungry again."*

One source of satisfaction she had in those days was school. She did well in the classroom, and she enjoyed the attention and honors she won in school. She also realized that the one way open to her for a better life was to get an education. In this ambition, she had her grandmother's support.

When Anna was thirteen, she went to Chicago and lived with her uncle. In Chicago, determined to get the best education she could, she lied about where she lived. In this way she was able to attend what she thought was the best high school in town. As a result of her academic performance, she won

---

*Anna Langford's story, as well as the story of thirteen other Black people, is related in more detail in the book, *Up From the Ghetto*, by Drotning and South.

a two-year scholarship to college. Visions of college and law school danced in her head. "From the time I was young," she said, "I was fascinated by the courtroom scenes in the movies. I always saw myself as the lawyer defending the poor and downtrodden." Fate intervened however, and Anna could not use her scholarship. Money was getting tight, so she had to get a job and help out at home. Using some office skills she had learned in high school, she got a job in an office.

But the desire to become a lawyer never left her. Eleven years later, she attended a speech given by Thurgood Marshall. After listening to Marshall, the first black man to become a U.S. Supreme Court Justice, she enrolled at Roosevelt University. Continuing to work to support herself, she attended college at night. Completing her program in three years, she enrolled in John Marshall Law School. She also got married at this time. One year later, her son was born, and motherhood forced her to drop out of law school. When her baby was three, she thought of going back to law school. "I realized that I would be thirty-nine years old before I got my law degree. I also realized, however, that in three years I would still be thirty-nine even if I didn't go back and finish my studies." So, at the age of thirty-nine, Mrs. Langford became a lawyer. Today, she works in a neighborhood law office, helping the poor and downtrodden that she had always dreamed of representing. She says, "There are no shortcuts to success. You need an education and you need to work hard. Luck plays a part in everyone's life, but if a person hasn't prepared himself, he will fail even when an opportunity presents itself. He will spend the rest of his days crying about how unlucky he is and how lucky someone else is."

Comprehension Questions

1. What was Anna Langford's goal, and what obstacles did she have to overcome to achieve this goal?

2. What role does she think luck plays in someone's life?

3. Come up with an example of how luck might pop up in people's lives but they can't take advantage of it because they are not prepared.

4. What are some examples of Mrs. Langford's fierce determination to succeed?

5. In your own words, explain the significance of the title.

Succeeding:
OVERCOMING THE ODDS

> *I intended to*
>
> *devote my full*
>
> *attention to*
>
> *figuring out the way*
>
> *to succeed. And I*
>
> *knew the first thing*
>
> *I would do. I would*
>
> *not let anybody else*
>
> *make the*
>
> *decisions.*

A POLITICAL FIRST

BARBARA JORDAN

WHEN BARBARA JORDAN was elected to the U.S. House of Representatives in 1972, she became the first African-American Congresswoman to come from the deep South. This was just one more first, in a series of firsts, in Barbara Jordan's life.

Barbara, the youngest of three girls, was born in Houston, Texas. Her father, a Baptist minister, supported his family by working as a warehouseman. A hard worker, her father expected his children to work hard, too. As a result, he ran a strict house and forbade entertainment like dancing and movies. In addition, he expected the girls to keep straight-A averages. Barbara always set equally high standards for herself. She said of her childhood, "We were poor, but so was everyone around us, so we did not notice it."

Living in a black ghetto and never seeing movies or television, Barbara was pretty much unaware of life outside her neighborhood. Although she knew she didn't want to do many of the things her mother had to do each day, she had no idea what she did want to do. This desire to do something different grew within her. She told a reporter from the *Washington Post*, "I wanted to be something unusual; I never wanted to be run-of-the-mill. For a while I thought about becoming a pharmacist. Then I thought, whoever heard of an outstanding pharmacist?" At the Phyllis Wheatley High School "Career Day" Assembly, Barbara heard Edith Sampson, a black lawyer from Chicago, speak. Listening to Ms. Sampson convinced Barbara to become a lawyer.

When Barbara graduated from Phyllis Wheatley High School in 1952, she ranked in the top 5 percent of her class. Enrolling at Texas Southern University, an all-black college in Houston, she majored in political science and history. She also ran unsuccessfully for president of the freshman class. A spellbinding orator, she led the debate team of Texas Southern to a series of championships. In 1956, she received her B.A. degree, *magna cum laude* (with great honors).

She applied and was admitted to Boston University Law School. At Boston

University she was shocked. "As good a student as I was in college, I never truly learned to think. I cannot describe what that did to my insides and my head. I thought, 'I'm being educated finally.' I realized, too, that the best training available in an all-black university *at that time* was *not* equal to the best training one developed at a white university. Separate was not equal; it just wasn't. I was doing sixteen years of remedial work in thinking." To catch up with her fellow students, Barbara spent many long nights reading in the University library. It was difficult. No one could have criticized her if she were to give up the task. Instead of giving up, however, she worked twice as hard.

After graduating from law school, Barbara returned to Houston. Lacking the money to rent an office, she started her practice in her parent's house. From a neighbor's chance remark, Barbara became involved in politics. After running for a seat in the Texas Senate and losing twice, she was determined to run a third time and not lose. She said, "I intended to devote my full attention to figuring out the way to succeed. And I knew the first thing I would do. I would not let anybody else make the decisions."

The third time she ran, Barbara was elected to the Texas State Senate. With this victory, she became the first African-American woman to sit as a Texas lawmaker. After two terms in the Texas Senate, she ran for and won a seat in the United States Congress. After an illustrious career in Congress, she announced that she would not run for a fourth term.

Following her own star, as she had done all her life, Barbara decided to teach political science at the University of Texas. When asked if she would ever return to politics, she indicated that "perhaps" she would, but at that time her heart was in her teaching. Barbara Jordan died in 1996 at the age of 59.

Comprehension Questions

1. What does the sentence, "She set equally high standards for herself" mean?

2. What qualities did Barbara Jordan have that helped her succeed?

3. Someone named Zig Ziglar, a motivational speaker, once said that a lot of things can stop you temporarily, but you are the only thing that can stop you permanently. How does that comment apply to Barbara Jordan?

4. As a child, what was her driving motivation?

5. In your own words, explain the significance of the title.

Succeeding:
OVERCOMING THE ODDS

> " Slowly, with
> determination and
> courage, he did
> turn things around. "

A Life-Changing Sacrifice

Bill Demby

BILL DEMBY. You may not remember his name, but if you saw the thirty-second commercial he starred in, you will never forget the man. The commercial was shot one hot, August day in New York City. A group of six African-American men are playing a fast-breaking, half-court basketball game on a city playground.

In appearance, this no-holds-barred game looks no different than any other game played that day in the city. Bill, a rugged looking man in his late thirties, goes up for a shot and is fouled hard by an opponent. As Bill falls flat on his back, the look on his face is one of anger and outrage, but also courage and determination. When the big man who had knocked Bill down extends a hand, one wonders if a lifetime of rivalry exists between these two aggressive competitors. The tension rises as he looks at his rival's outstretched hand. Then, Bill gets to his feet. Just as you begin to notice something odd-looking about Bill's legs, a voice on the commercial says:

> *"When Bill Demby was in Vietnam, he dreamed of coming home and playing a little basketball—a dream that all but died when he lost both legs to a Viet Cong rocket. Then researchers discovered that DuPont plastic could make truly lifelike artificial limbs. Now Bill's back, and some say he hasn't lost a step."*

You sit there amazed—amazed at the technology that developed these plastic and foam legs and feet. You are more amazed, however, at the man who uses them as well as if they were his own limbs.

Demby, a poor country boy, was picking cotton at age five so he could get money to buy clothes. A star basketball player in high school, he hoped to play college basketball and then go on to the pros. When told he wasn't college material, however, he went to work in a battery factory. Drafted into the army in 1970, he was sent to Vietnam. In Vietnam, his dream of playing basketball was shattered when a truck he was driving was hit by an enemy rocket.

The twenty-year-old army private never saw it coming. "It was like a mortar hit the side of my door. All I remember is smoke filling the truck, and I saw my left leg on the floor." Demby was transported by helicopter to the 95th Evacuation Hospital. There, minutes later, with his left leg already severed below the knee, doctors amputated his right leg. His foot had been so badly crushed, it would make the leg useless.

After spending a year at Walter Reed Army Hospital, Demby was released from the army. Readjustment to civilian life without his legs was tough for Demby. In this period, he developed problems with alcohol and dangerous drugs. He hit bottom when he passed out on his mother's sofa one night. "When I woke, I found my mother and sister clutching each other and crying. They told me I had said I was going to kill somebody. That's when I decided to turn things around."

It was through sports that Demby made it back. First, he began playing wheelchair basketball and then he became a ski instructor for the disabled. It was while playing wheelchair basketball that he and others were approached by DuPont to try out the company's new artificial legs. Later, he was selected from this group to make the commercial. Slowly, with determination and courage, he did turn things around. Today, he teaches skiing to disabled people and participates in track and field events, as well as regular and wheelchair basketball. Demby, realizing that fame in television is fleeting, speaks of the time when no one will remember his name, and that certainly will happen. But as an inspiration and symbol of bravery and strength no one who has seen that commercial or heard this story will forget the man.

Comprehension Questions

1. What makes Bill Demby a hero and an inspiration?

2. The commercial brought Bill fame and some money, but how had he prepared for this bit of luck?

3. To be successful, what non-physical obstacle did he have to overcome?

4. In your own words, explain the significance of the title.

Succeeding:
OVERCOMING THE ODDS

> "
> *At this point, I*
> *could see life in*
> *perspective. I had*
> *learned a tough*
> *lesson about the*
> *importance of an*
> *education.*
> "

EDUCATION COUNTS

BYRON DEAN TOLSON

BYRON DEAN TOLSON, an all-state basketball player at Central High School in Kansas City, MO, got his dream. After playing basketball for four years at the University of Arkansas, he was the fifth round pick of the Seattle Super Sonics in the 1974 NBA draft. Of the thousands of young men who have this dream each year, he was one of the few who had his dream come true. But there is an old saying that comes to mind, "You have to be careful what you dream for, because you just might get it."

You don't need an education if you are going to play pro ball; everyone knows that. That's probably why Byron Dean Tolson didn't go to classes in his senior year at the University of Arkansas. As a result, he was suspended from the school. The fact that he didn't have a degree, however, did not stop the Sonics from signing him to a contract. When he left the University, however, a degree was not the only thing he was lacking; he did not have an education either. In fact, he had graduated from high school and spent four years at college without ever being able to read or write.

In 1977, as he started his fourth year in pro ball, Dean bought a $200,000 home and parked his new Mercedes in the driveway. Six games into the season, the Sonics cut Dean from the team. For the next six years he played professional ball anywhere in the world that he could get a job. At the age of thirty-two, however, it was over; he was finished. In a *Sports Illustrated* article, he explained how he felt at the time. "No one knows what it's like to be recognized all your life for something. To be recognized as a basketball star—to be somebody—and then, to no longer have that. You're a zero." He explained how he had played and was applauded by hundreds of thousands of fans all over the world. "But when my career was over, I was worth $3.50 an hour. That's all. Do you know how much that hurts?"

Unable to read or write, Dean looked back on his years in school. From the start, as a 6' 4" high school center, Dean was a successful athlete. As a result of his success in basketball, however, he lost perspective. "I didn't do any school work. I hated every class." He believes that the only reason he graduated from high school was because the coach pressured teachers to pass him. More likely, though, as bad a student as he was, there were probably others in his class who were worse. As a result, he passed each course with the minimum passing grade.

At the University, his attitude toward academics did not change, nor did his grades. By the time he was finally suspended from the University in his senior year, he had gotten more than fifteen Fs. The courses he had received credit for were subjects like golf, tennis, and dancing. In moments of bitterness, he blamed the coaches and high school teachers who passed him each year even though he could not read.

With nothing to look forward to but a life of dead-end jobs at minimum pay, life looked bleak. It was then, at the age of thirty-two, he decided to get an education. Fortunately, thanks to the Razorback Foundation, Dean was able to get some financial aid to return to Arkansas. A bigger obstacle facing him was his lack of basic skills. The first year back, he studied nine hours a day. Even with all that time spent studying, however, he was still doing poorly. The material was still too difficult for him. He insisted that he needed a tutor, but there was very little money available for that. No one but Dean believed he had any chance of ever getting a degree. "At this point, I could see life in perspective. I had learned a tough lesson about the importance of an education." He resolved that this time it was going to be different. He would never miss a test, never cut a class, always get his assignments in on time, and get to know the professors.

For most people, a burning ambition to reach an important goal that is clearly important and an action plan to follow would have been enough. Dean, however, had wasted too many years and had failed to master too many basics. When he needed help the most, he was fortunate to find Marcia Harriel as a tutor. Sacrificing everything, including sleep sometimes, Dean worked fifteen hours a day, seven days a week. Finally, in 1988, at the age of thirty-six, the University of Arkansas awarded Byron Dean Tolson a Bachelor of Science degree in Education. One suspects that this is one teacher who will not let a student who doesn't do the work slip by.

Comprehension Questions

1. When he was thirty-two, why did life seem so empty for Dean?

2. If you had a brother or sister who was traveling the same path that Byron Dean Tolson took through high school, what would you tell him or her?

3. When Dean says that in high school "he lost perspective," what does he mean?

4. As a result of situations like Byron Dean Tolson's, the NCAA, which controls college athletics, wrote a new rule in 1989. Colleges are no longer permitted to give a scholarship to any high school athlete who does not have at least a "C" average in high school and a score of 700 on the Scholastic Aptitude Test. In addition, Division I colleges require the high school applicant for an athletic scholarship to have at least a "C" average in eleven full academic courses. How would this rule have hurt Dean Tolson if it was in effect in 1974?

5. In your own words, explain the significance of the title.

Succeeding:
OVERCOMING THE ODDS

"

...because of his

dedication to a

cause, he stands

number one in the

hearts of millions

of people.

"

THE PROUD FIGHT

CAESAR CHAVEZ

OF CAESAR CHAVEZ, Robert F. Kennedy said, "He is one of the heroic figures of our time." Like other people we feature in these pages, Caesar Chavez started with less than nothing. However, unlike some of the others, Chavez never became wealthy or achieved a great deal in the way of material success. Yet, because of his dedication to a cause, he stands number one in the hearts of millions of people.

Caesar Chavez was one of five children born on a farm in Arizona. When the Depression hit, the Chavez family was forced off their farm. Like thousands of other homeless people at the time, they went on the road and became migrant workers. Like thousands of others, they followed the sun, harvesting crops from Arizona to California. By the time he dropped out of school in the eighth grade, he had attended more than thirty elementary schools. Despite all the schools he had attended, or maybe because of them, he could barely read or write. Later, when he realized how illiteracy held his people back, he taught himself to read and write.

Chavez remembers the poor treatment of migrant children in these schools: "The schools treated you like you didn't exist. Their indifference was incredible. But even some teachers who cared, tried to get you to eliminate your native language. When students did speak in Spanish, they were sometimes punished."

In an article in the *New Republic*, Martin Duberman summarized Chavez's early days. "He remembers walking barefoot to school through the mud and fishing in the canals for wild mustard greens to ward off starvation. He remembers, too, collecting tinfoil from empty cigarette packages to sell to a junk dealer for a sweatshirt or a pair of shoes. His parents, he recalls, got up at 5:30 in the morning during the Depression to go pick peas all day in the fields. Then, they did not earn the seventy cents to pay the cost of their transportation. Living under bridges for protection against weather and being forcibly ejected by the police from the 'Anglo' section of a movie theater are also part of his memories. Most bitterly of all, he remembers working seven days a week picking wine grapes only to have the contractor disappear with his pay."

Discharged from the U.S. Navy after serving during World War II, Chavez returned to migrant farm work. He came back to the tarpaper shacks without running water or indoor plumbing. It was during this period that he began his fight to improve the life of the migrant farm worker. In 1951, Chavez became a community labor organizer. In 1958, he became director of the Community Service Organization. Then, in 1962, he resigned his position because he thought that the organization was not doing enough for poor farm workers. With his wife Helen, who took a job to help support their growing family, Chavez started the National Farm Workers Association. To do this, he had to withdraw $1,200 from their bank account. This was the only money they had in the world. During this time, he did not always have enough money to feed himself and his family. As a result, Chavez began begging food from the workers he visited on his organizing tours. "It turned out to be about the best thing I could have done, although at first it's hard on your pride. Some of our best members came in that way. If people give you their food, they'll give you their hearts."

Gradually, however, his union grew larger and began to sign labor contracts with the vineyards. For the first time, migrant workers got the rights denied them for so long. While the plight of the migrant workers was far from over, Chavez and the union had taken the first big step. For the next twenty-five years, Chavez kept the plight of the migrant worker and his cause in the eyes and conscience of the American people. Chavez died in 1993.

Comprehension Questions

1. What motivated Caesar Chavez to do something with his life?

2. What obstacles did he have to overcome?

3. What prompted him to quit a good job and return to a life of poverty?

4. What enabled him to succeed?

5. In your own words, explain the significance of the title.

Succeeding:
OVERCOMING THE ODDS

> "
> *You devote yourself*
> *to getting an*
> *education and a*
> *profession when you*
> *are young, then for*
> *the rest of your life,*
> *you get the benefits*
> *of your hard work.*
> "

A JOURNEY
TO SUCCESS

Chau Tran

WHEN CHAU GOT off the plane in California, she spoke very little English. In fact, all she could say was, "Hello, my name is Chau. I am eleven." Chau eventually graduated from the University of California with high honors. It was a long, tough journey, but the first ten years were the most difficult.

With her mother, father, and brother, Chau climbed into an already overcrowded fishing boat. Setting sail on a dark, moonless night was not an accident. If a Vietnamese patrol boat spotted them, the best they could hope for was to be sent home without any of their possessions. The worst that could happen, no one wanted to think about. As they neared the coast of Indonesia, they were in the greatest danger, for pirates, cruel and ruthless men, preyed on these boat people. After killing the men and taking any worldly possessions the refugees might have, the pirates tortured and killed the woman and children. The boat Chau and her family were on was more fortunate than many earlier boats. Chau's boat reached Indonesia safely. From there, they were transported to a refugee camp in Singapore. Three months later, with the help of a refugee organization, they landed in California. With little more than the clothes on their backs and a strong desire to make a better life for themselves and their children, the Tran family entered the mainstream of American life.

Although Chau had not been in a regular classroom in three years and spoke very little English, she enrolled in the local elementary school. Seven years later, she was the valedictorian of her high school graduating class. When asked the secret of her success, she responds, "Hard work. Five nights a week I spent a minimum of three hours per night doing my homework. I reserved Sunday afternoons for beginning work on projects like book reports or science projects."

She admits, for the most part, she enjoyed doing homework. She enjoyed the satisfaction of mastering something, and she enjoyed getting good grades. "Literature, however, was sometimes frustrating," she said, "because of the shades of meanings in words. No matter how hard I tried, I would miss things in the stories."

But even if the classes were boring or the work difficult, Chau never let up. "My parents," she said, "sacrificed very much for my brother and me. My father, a teacher in Vietnam, could get very little work. In those early days, my family was so poor that each night my mother washed the clothes we wore that day for the next day. Now it is up to my brother and me to fulfill our parents' dreams for us. My father always told us, 'the worst failure is not to try. If you try but don't succeed, that's learning.' If I didn't try my best, I would feel that I was letting my family down. I would feel that I was laughing in the face of their sacrifices for me."

Three months later, Chau, a very pretty young woman, went on her first date. "I promised my parents I would not date until I was twenty-one. In high school and college I was asked to go out, but I always refused. Most of the boys understood why I could not go out with them." But she has no regrets about that. "The girls I knew in high school who dated," she explains, "only went out two or three times a month on dates. They spent the rest of the month, however, thinking and talking about boys. I see the benefits that come from an education. You devote yourself to getting an education and a profession when you are young, then for the rest of your life, you get the benefits of your hard work. It's like the story of the ant and the grasshopper. Because the ant worked hard in the summer, he comfortably survived the winter. The grasshopper, who lazily wasted the summer, starved in the winter. I'm no genius. I am just a hard worker. If I could do well at school, anyone could."

Comprehension Questions

1. What was the biggest obstacle Chau had to overcome once she was in this country?

2. How did the story of the ant and the grasshopper that she used apply to her life?

3. Why does Chau suggest that dating interferes with a young person's education?

4. In your own words, explain the significance of the title.

Succeeding:
OVERCOMING THE ODDS

" *...his story of*

courage and

determination

in the face of

overwhelming odds

will always live on. "

HIS LEFT FOOT

CHRISTY BROWN

C HRISTY BROWN, whose biography, *My Left Foot,* was made into a movie, was born in Dublin, Ireland, in 1933. At the time, doctors did not understand how the lack of oxygen at birth affected infants. When his lifeless, blue body was brought into the world, they diagnosed him as mentally defective. His mother, however, convinced that he was not an imbecile, began to work with him. Each day she read to young Christy and spoke to him, but she never got a response.

Christy, doctors later would learn, had a form of cerebral palsy, which appeared to leave his entire body paralyzed. In effect, he could not move a muscle nor respond in any way. Although her husband helped with the baby, Christy consumed most of his mother's time. Because they had seven other children to look after, relatives suggested they put Christy in an institution. Neither the mother nor father could do this.

Christy described those years as living in a strange dream. He could see and hear everything going on around him, but there was no way he could let them know this. One day when he was five, Christy sat on the kitchen floor watching his sister Mona write on a chalkboard. Suddenly, his left foot shot out. He grasped the chalk between his toes and scribbled wildly across the slate. He had never used his foot before. Christy looked up to find everyone staring at him. Mrs. Brown understood at once. She kneeled at his side. "I'll show you what to do with it, Chris." She drew the letter *A*, "Copy it, Christy," she said.

He strained to make his foot work. Nothing. He tried again. A crooked line. That was all. Again he tried. He knew he must keep trying. He had drawn one wobbly side to the *A* and half of the other when the chalk snapped. In anger and frustration, he was ready to toss the chalk away. His mother's quiet encouragement, however, calmed him. Finally, straining every muscle, he did it. He drew the letter *A!* He saw his mother smiling, tears shining on her cheeks. Then there was a great shout, and he was whirled up onto his father's shoulders.

Within the year, Christy learned to print the whole alphabet by holding the chalk between his toes. From this beginning, he was able to learn how to read and write. He also developed a set of printed symbols that allowed him to communicate with his family by language. Gaining a little more control of his muscles, he began to pull himself around the room and up and down stairs.

When his father built a cart from some old carriage wheels, he was even able to get around outside. On these trips, he was pulled by one of his brothers. When the cart broke, he fell into a deep depression. Gradually, however, he came out of the depression when he became interested in painting with watercolors. When he was able to lose himself in his painting, he forgot his pain and loneliness. Shortly after this, he began to write.

A clinic for cerebral palsied children opened in Dublin when he was eighteen. The doctors there thought they might be able to help Christy gain control over some more of his muscles. They prescribed exercises and activities for him. But try as he might, he could make no progress. He came to realize that he would never be able to have a physical body that was just like everyone else's. Reading, writing, and thinking, however, were things he could do. At that moment he decided to write his own life story. He wrote *My Left Foot*. Then he went on to write four more novels and three books of poetry. Most fulfilling of all, perhaps, was meeting and falling in love with a woman. In 1972, Christy and Ann married. Although Christy was to die nine years later at the age of forty-nine, his story of courage and determination in the face of overwhelming odds will always live on. Whenever anyone is ready to give up because life is hard, he or she has only to think of the young boy who could move only his left foot.

Comprehension Questions

1. If Christy had not suffered from a lack of oxygen at birth, he would have had a normal body. If he had a normal body, do you think he would have become a famous writer?

2. Psychologists claim that most people use only a small percentage (20%) of their talents. Christy clearly used close to 100% of his talent. What percentage of your talent are you using?

3. What do you suppose some of the things are that hold people back from using more of their talents?

4. In your own words, explain the significance of the title.

Succeeding:
OVERCOMING THE ODDS

" *I thank all of whom insisted that I grow up to make something of myself.* "

"NOTHING GOOD COMES EASY"

CLARENCE THOMAS

BORN IN A segregated Georgia port city, Clarence Thomas knew
hardship and prejudice first-hand. Shortly after Clarence was born,
his father deserted the family. His mother, who, in good times,
worked for minimum wage preparing crabs, struggled on. The house they
lived in had no running water and only an outdoor toilet, which had to be
shared with several other families on the block. Food, which was hard to get,
was always scarce during the off-season at the crab factory. Shoes were worn
only to school so they would not wear out too quickly. Clarence's mother
recalls, "Where we came from, we didn't have anything. We just lived day by
day. It was at this point that my father and my mother stepped in to help us."
Mrs. Williams says that her son's nomination to the Supreme Court proves
that hard work pays off. "Nothing good comes easy; Clarence knows that. He
has lived it."

At the age of six, Clarence and his sister went to live with their grandparents.
This proved to be an important point in his life. Thomas later related that
his grandfather was the single greatest influence in his life. His grandfather
emphasized the necessity of getting good grades in school and the importance
of hard work. A typical day for young Clarence started by leaving home early
to go to school. When he returned home, he worked six more hours for his
grandfather and then spent several more hours each night doing homework.

His grandfather's lessons of hard work, self-reliance, and the importance
of education were reinforced at the school to which his grandfather sent him,
a black elementary school taught by white, Catholic nuns. The nuns instilled
in Clarence both a faith in God and a faith in himself. They expected that
he and the other students would give the best they had in them. In this, the
students rarely disappointed the nuns. After a few years, his sister returned
to live with his mother, but Thomas stayed on at his grandparents. Today,

his sister picks crabs for minimum wage just as his mother did. She is justly proud of her brother. Of his sister, to whom he is still close, he says, "She could never see the value of education. She never really applied herself at school."

While still living at his grandfather's house, Thomas went to the local Catholic High School. There, his pattern of putting 100% into everything he did paid off. As a result, he was both a student athlete and an honor student. Thomas was awarded a full scholarship to Holy Cross College in Boston based on his high school academic record. His hard work and accomplishments at Holy Cross enabled him to enroll in and graduate from Yale University Law School.

Notified of his nomination to the country's highest court, Thomas made an inspirational speech. "As a child, I could not dare dream that I would ever see the Supreme Court, not to mention be nominated to it. In my view, only in America could this have been possible. I thank all of those who helped me along the way. I thank all who have helped me to this point and this moment in my life, especially my grandparents, my mother, and the nuns. I thank all of whom insisted that I grow up to make something of myself. I hope to be an example to those who are where I was. I hope to show them that, indeed, there is hope."

Thomas has proven that the American Dream is still possible for a "dirt-poor" boy or girl. As a teacher remarked, "Clarence could be just as proud and happy as a priest, teacher, plumber, or as a judge. Unlike many people, he made the most of the talents that God gave him. That is what we all have to do."

Comprehension Questions

1. What qualities enabled Thomas to reach the level of success that he did?

2. Why did Thomas succeed in getting a good career, while his sister did not?

3. To get to where he is today, what do you suppose Clarence Thomas had to give up in his earlier years?

4. Why was it an advantage for him to be in a school where everybody worked hard?

5. In your own words, explain the significance of the title.

Succeeding:
OVERCOMING THE ODDS

> "
>
> *I realized I could*
>
> *do what I wanted.*
>
> *I could turn*
>
> *square now, even*
>
> *straighten up if*
>
> *I wanted to.*
>
> "

STOLEN YEARS

CLAUDE BROWN

C LAUDE BROWN'S parents came to New York City from South Carolina. The family lived in a Harlem tenement at 146th Street and Eighth Avenue, where Claude, his younger brother, and his two sisters grew up. In New York, his father worked for the railroad, and his mother worked as a domestic servant.

Even before he was of school age, Claude Brown—known as "Sonny" to his friends—was living in the streets. Fighting and stealing were a way of life for him. He began to build the type of reputation needed for survival in the ghetto. When he was eight, he was sent to Bellevue Hospital for psychiatric observation. Within the next two years he had made a name for himself in the infamous Harlem gang, the Buccaneers.

Among the boys in the gang, there was a smaller group who called themselves *The Forty Thieves*. This group lived up to its name. In his autobiography, *Manchild in the Promised Land*, Brown states that he was a child delinquent because he wanted to be one, because he had an "uncontrollable urge to steal." He recognized, too, that it gave him "a sort of social status." By the time he was ten, Sonny had a long record of truancy. His record included running away from the city children's center and several expulsions from school. His bent for trouble caused his relatives to comment that he must have been "born with the devil in him." Hoping that a change of scene might straighten him out, his family sent him to the South to stay on a farm with grandparents and an aunt.

Within a year, Claude was back in New York and in trouble again. At the age of eleven, he was sent to the Wiltwyck School for emotionally disturbed and deprived boys. He remained there for two years. A major influence on him at the school was psychologist and director, Dr. Ernest Papanek. Brown has said that Papanek "was probably the smartest and the deepest guy I had ever met. He knew how to answer the hard questions without lying." Brown also met Mrs. Eleanor Roosevelt, the founder of Wiltwyck School. Although

53

he later dedicated his book to her, at the time his reaction to her was one of wonder. "How," he asked, "did the President have time to bother with this crazy-acting old lady?"

Despite these positive influences, when Brown returned to Harlem, he went back to his old way of life in the streets. At this point, he began selling and using marijuana. A bullet wound that he received at thirteen while stealing sheets from a clothesline built up his reputation among his peers. At fourteen, he was sent to the Warwick Reform School for the first of his three terms there. Among his chief influences at Warwick was the wife of the school's superintendent, Mrs. Alfred A. Cohen. It was Mrs. Cohen who started Brown reading biographies of African-American celebrities, as well as those of selected white men like Einstein and Schweitzer.

At the age of sixteen, Brown was released from Warwick for what would be the last time. At the outset, he took a straight job because he had to satisfy the parole requirements. In a few months, however, he quit the job and went back to being a street hustler. During a drug deal, an addict robbed him of the drugs he was carrying. Brown knew what was expected of him. He would lose respect if he did not get a gun and go after the man. Although he didn't want to do this, he set out to do what he thought must be done. When the police arrested the man for some other crime, Brown felt very relieved. In a strange way, this marked a turning point in his life. Brown said he had come to realize several truths. "I realized I could do what I wanted. I could turn square now, even straighten up if I wanted to. I'd been through the street-life thing."

A second realization that came to him was that women controlled the political process in Harlem. They did so, he concluded, because a large percentage of men in Harlem had police records. This effectively barred them from having any say in the political future of Harlem.

To make something of himself, he decided he needed an education. At the age of sixteen, the boy they couldn't keep in school enrolled in night school. To support himself, Brown worked as a busboy, shipping clerk, deliveryman, postal clerk, and bookkeeper. At seventeen, he moved to Greenwich Village where he joined a group of jazz musicians. Later he bought a piano and practiced as much as eight hours a day. "For the first time," he recalled, "I felt as though I was really doing things."

After getting his high school diploma, Brown returned to Harlem. Looking around he saw that many of his old friends were either dead or in prison. A few, however, had managed to escape the trap. For example, his brother, a drug addict who had been in jail for armed robbery, got himself straightened out and was attending college. Brown decided to do the same. Four years later, Brown graduated from college and enrolled in law school. In turning around his life the way he had, Claude Brown is an inspiration. For those who feel they may have wasted the first sixteen years of their life, Brown is proof that where there is a will, there is a way to change.

Comprehension Questions

1. What does the phrase *Where there's a will, there's a way* mean, and how does it apply to Claude Brown?

2. Claude's parents probably had as much money as anyone else in their neighborhood. Why, then, did Claude take up a life of crime?

3. To succeed in life as an honest citizen, what obstacles did Claude have to overcome?

4. What satisfaction did Claude find in the straight life?

5. In your own words, explain the significance of the title.

Succeeding:
OVERCOMING THE ODDS

"Never had I felt so challenged nor so determined to make something of myself."

"THE MEASURE OF A MAN"

DANIEL INOUYE

THE LIFE STORY of Daniel Inouye, war hero, lawyer, and United States Senator from Hawaii, reads like a novel. The first son of a poor, immigrant Japanese farmer, Inouye enlisted in the United States Army at the outbreak of World War II. Sent overseas as a corporal in the famous 442 Regimental Combat Team, which was made up of only Japanese-Americans, Inouye won a battlefield commission and many medals. He lost his right arm, however, to a German grenade. After he returned home, he went to college, then to law school, and then on to Congress and the U. S. Senate. But earlier, when he entered tenth grade, Daniel Inouye had no idea what he wanted to do with the rest of his life.

In his autobiography, *Journey To Washington*, Daniel tells the story of his high school days. MacKinley High, due to a subtle system of segregation, was an all-Japanese high school. For this reason, students and staff called it, as a joke, Tokyo High. While careful never to be caught by his friends studying or doing homework, Daniel liked school and did fairly well. In the tenth grade, however, he was somewhat disappointed when he was separated from his friends and put in the highest tenth grade class. While all the students in the class were *nisei* (American citizens of Japanese descent) like himself, he saw he was different. He found himself "with a breed of kids who kept trying to pretend that their skin was white and their eyes were blue. I was surrounded by all those starched white shirts and shined shoes. Here I was, a poor boy who didn't like to wear shoes."

Despite his classmates, Daniel enjoyed the class and did well, so well, in fact, that his teacher recommended him for the high school honor society. Although he did not show it, he was proud that he had been recommended; his parents were even more proud. Before being admitted, however, he had to be interviewed and voted upon by a panel of senior students.

In the interview, Daniel expected to be quizzed on his knowledge of history, science, or math. Therefore, he was surprised when the first question asked, by a senior, was, "Why don't you wear shoes?" He responded, "Because I only have one pair and they have to last."

The rest of the questions were of a similar nature. In effect, they criticized the clothes he wore and the people with whom he was friends. Daniel quickly realized that he was not going to be allowed to join this organization. He explained, "There was no racial prejudice connected with my rejection. In fact, the four senior students who rejected me, were themselves of Japanese ancestry. Rather, they rejected me because I would not pretend to be white and imitate the white man's way." The most difficult part for Daniel lay ahead: he had to tell his mother and father he was rejected for membership; however, he couldn't tell them the real reason, because they would have blamed themselves for his rejection.

While he felt pain and humiliation at the time, he also recognized that some good had come out of it. "The interview with the committee left me enraged and a little confused. Most of all, though, it left me with a burning need to '*show those guys!*' Never had I felt so challenged nor so determined to make something of myself. As a matter of fact, I don't think it's unfair to say that those four snobbish seniors are at least partly responsible for whatever successes I subsequently enjoyed. Their faces stuck in my mind and do to this day. For years afterward, I charged at every obstacle in my path as though those four had personally put it there. It was absolutely essential for me to overcome the obstacles, to prove that shoes and neckties were no measure of a man."

The boy who started tenth grade with no idea of the future or what he wanted to do with his life, now had a burning resolve. Over the course of the next twenty years, he showed not only those boys, but also the rest of the country what the true measure of a man is.

Comprehension Questions

1. What incident proved to be a turning point in Daniel Inouye's life and why?

2. The last sentence implies that how people look or dress is not how they should be measured or judged. How should a person be judged?

3. While he was in U. S. Army hospital, Daniel set a goal to become a politician because he thought that it was the best way to change things in society for the better. What obstacles do you suppose he had to overcome to reach his goal?

4. In your own words, explain the significance of the title.

Succeeding:
OVERCOMING THE ODDS

"By not running away from his responsibilities…he made both a successful career and a successful life for himself and his family."

THE RIGHT CHOICE

DANNY AIELLO

WHEN HE WAS nominated for an Academy Award for his role in *"Do The Right Thing,"* Danny Aiello had reached the top of his profession. But the road to a life of fame and success was a tough one. He could have just as easily wound up in prison rather than Hollywood.

When he was five, his father walked out on the family, but even when his father had been there, life was hard for the family; after he left, it became even tougher. Although his mother earned a little money sewing, the family had to go on welfare to survive. At the age of seven, to do his part, Danny went out on the streets of New York City. There he shined shoes and sold newspapers. After completing eighth grade, he dropped out of school to get whatever full-time job he could. While doing his part for the family, though, he was also getting into trouble.

"I had a great deal of violence in me for a long time. As a result, I was always getting into fights. When I was twelve, my friends and I started a gang. We were into theft and gang fighting. Between the fighting and skipping school, I was getting into a lot of trouble. I never held anyone up, but I was once shot in the leg with a zip gun. I knew it was only a matter of time before things got really bad."

Seeing the army as a way out, Danny, who was then only sixteen, lied about his age and joined the army. After serving three years in Germany, Danny returned home; shortly after that, he got married and started his family. While the marriage helped settled him down, this was not an easy time for him and his wife. He was Italian and his wife was Jewish, so neither family accepted their marriage. In addition, he still had not been able to get a steady job.

In 1957, things started looking up when Danny got a job at Greyhound Bus Lines, but in 1967, because of his involvement with a wildcat strike, he was fired. For a married man with three children, not having a job can be a crushing blow, and in many instances can cause the breakup of the family.

Despite his fears though, Danny showed persistence. He says, "I always had a fear of not being able to take care of my family, of not having my children look up to me. I was always afraid of my family being homeless and one of my children asking me one day why I couldn't keep a roof over our heads."

One day it almost came to pass. "When we had to go on welfare, it was very embarrassing to me." It was shortly after this, however, that he got a job in a New York nightclub as a bouncer. When the owner of the club took a night off, Danny acted as emcee. He found that he liked being on stage. As a result, he began trying out for parts on the Broadway stage. Like everyone else who wants to act, Danny, was rejected for many parts, but finally he began to get some small parts. As he worked at acting, he knew that being unemployed was always just around the corner. With his success in "*Do The Right Thing*," however, he got some breathing space.

Of his life, Aiello says, "I want to be an inspiration to kids, but I don't want them to get the wrong message. I don't want kids to hear that I didn't go to school and then think, 'Well, he left school and now he's famous, so I can drop out, and I can become famous.' I hesitate to give that information, but I have to because this is my life; this is what I did."

As Aiello points out, times are different now and dropping out of school is not the way to succeed. As someone who started with nothing and kept trying, even when things got bad, Aiello could be anyone's role model. By not running away from his responsibilities to his family and going after his dream, he made both a successful career and a successful life for himself and his family. Today, he is surrounded by his family and reaping the rewards of his labor.

Comprehension Questions

1. Some people might think that Danny's first break in show business as an emcee was luck, and in some ways it might have been. In what way, though, wasn't it luck?

2. How did he work to capitalize on his luck?

3. Although he grew up in New York, Danny, as a young person, never dreamed of being a successful actor. How did wealth and success as an actor come to him?

4. What obstacles did Danny have to overcome to be a success?

5. How did he break out of his environment?

6. In your own words, explain the significance of the title.

Succeeding:
OVERCOMING THE ODDS

> "...courage, and determination in the face of an overwhelming physical handicap is unconquerable."

"JUST LIKE EVERYONE ELSE"

EARL SCHENCK MIERS

EARL MIERS' BIRTH was a difficult one. It was a breech delivery, which means the baby's head is not positioned to come out first. As a result, the baby must be repositioned before it can be born. In the meantime, the baby suffers from a lack of oxygen. In effect, the baby is suffocated. Thus, when Earl Miers was born, he was alive, but barely.

As a result of the lack of oxygen, the baby was blue. Although the doctors rushed to put the baby on oxygen, too much time had elapsed. Permanent brain damage had already occurred, and Earl Miers was inflicted with a type of cerebral palsy. What this meant in practical terms, Miers described in his autobiography, *The Trouble Bush*: "The day began for me as though I were trying to thread a needle on a moving train. My arms shook and I had a speech impediment. When I drank liquids, the glass had to be held for me. At mealtime, my meat had to be cut for me. Even my hair had to be combed."

At the time Miers was growing up in the 1930's, medical science was ignorant on the subject of brain damage. Unfortunately, superstition filled the gap. Neighbors looked upon "the shakes" as a punishment from God. Doctors were almost as bad in their diagnosis. Miers recalls that the doctors took a simple approach, "Keep the bowels open and make the child take long periods of rest in a room with the shades drawn. As though there were something especially nerve-wracking in clouds, blue sky, and a child's soaring imagination."

Unfortunately, many parents did not know what to do with their children, either. Some, in effect, withdrew their child from life. Hiding the child away in an institution or at home, the parents did not prepare the child for life. Other parents, hoping to find a miracle cure, subjected their child to endless experiments. Miers was lucky in this. Although his mother had gone in search of miracle cures, his father was wiser. Accepting his son's limitations from the beginning, he prepared Earl for life. He taught the boy that he might "in some things just have to depend on other people. But in any case you must live and grow up just like everyone else."

His mother once had a big argument with a school principal. The principal insisted, "A child like this belongs in an institution." Mrs. Miers, however, enrolled her son in the school. Learning to read quickly, he became almost at once a student of history. "It was as though all of my grandmother's ancestors whispered to me how they had reacted to events gone by." The grandmother to whom he referred was his father's mother. Her favorite subject of conversation were the stories her grandparents had told her. These stories were about their experience during the Revolutionary War. She also had her own story about the time Abraham Lincoln shook her hand.

Unable to control a pencil, Earl carried a typewriter from class to class in school. "Arithmetic became my favorite subject," he recalled. "Only a cerebral-palsied child who has learned how to add and subtract on a typewriter can explain why. The effort to shift the carriage in order to correct a single decimal point becomes too exhausting to make a mistake." Every Friday afternoon he lugged the heavy typewriter the two miles back to his home. It was needed by the Mohawk Stamp Company, which was a part-time, mail-order business set up by his father.

During this period, Earl became an eager reader. "Sometimes I read three or four books in a day," Miers wrote in his autobiography. "I read and read and knew that I had to write." The first stories typed out by Earl on his old typewriter were published in "Tribe," a paper of the Lone Scouts of America, a national boys' organization to which he belonged. Before he was fifteen, he was selling short pieces to *The Country Gentleman, Wallace's Farm Weekly*, and other magazines. When he was a junior in high school, he became a reporter for the *Bergen Evening Record*. After graduating from high school, he joined the staff of another paper

Having saved $1,800, Earl entered Rutgers University as a journalism major. At Rutgers, he became editor-in-chief of the *Targum*, the campus newspaper. In addition he served as campus correspondent for *The Newark Evening News, The Bergen Evening Record*, and *The New York Times*. He also met and wooed his wife, who had been a student at the New Jersey College for Women.

From that point on, his life was filled with predictable, although in no sense easy, successes. But if Earl Schenck Miers had been only one tenth as successful as he was, he still would have proved that the human spirit, courage, and determination in the face of an overwhelming physical handicap is unconquerable.

Comprehension Questions

1. Explain the meaning of the first sentence in the last paragraph. Specifically, why would his successes be predictable?

2. If you could choose to have either the best athletic ability in the class or the best mind, which would you choose? If that had been Earl Miers' choice, what do you suppose he would have chosen?

3. On a scale of 1 to 10, with 10 being the highest, how would you rate these qualities in yourself? Make a comment for each grade you give yourself.

    1   2   3   4   5   6   7   8   9   1 0
    Determination - You can make a firm resolve to get something done and do it.
    Comment:

    1   2   3   4   5   6   7   8   9   1 0
    Persistence - Once you start a job you stay with it until it's finished.
    Comment:

    1   2   3   4   5   6   7   8   9   1 0
    Willingness to Work Hard - You are willing to tackle a tough job and make sacrifices in order to get it done.
    Comment:

    1   2   3   4   5   6   7   8   9   1 0
    Ability to meet obstacles and overcome them - You strive to win despite the odds.
    Comment:

4. In your own words, explain the significance of the title.

Succeeding:
OVERCOMING THE ODDS

"

You can choose to be

happy and work

at life, or you

can choose to be

miserable and

give up on it.

"

FROM POVERTY TO HOLLYWOOD

EDWARD JAMES OLMOS

WHAT IS SUCCESS? For Edward James Olmos, the star of *"Stand And Deliver"* and *"Miami Vice,"* it is doing what you like to do and doing it well. "Sure," he says, "as a successful actor, I have money and fame. And if I wasn't selective about the parts I took, I suppose I could have a lot more money and fame. But money and fame, in themselves, can't make you happy. You don't have to leave L.A. to see plenty of rich, but unhappy people."

Nor do we have to look hard to see that Olmos puts his money where his mouth is. He turned down a major role in the sure money-winner *"Scarface,"* to make a film called *"The Ballad Of Gregorio Cortez."* "It is a story that needed telling," he says. "It is a true story about an innocent Mexican cowboy who was hunted by the Texas Rangers. He was one of the few heroes of Latin ancestry shown on the screen."

Olmos is quick to tell the young people in trouble to whom he talks, that he wasn't born rich and famous. In fact, the Mexican-American actor, who didn't speak English until he started school, tells them, "I started out just like you." Until he was seven, he lived in a three-room house with eleven members of his family; the kitchen even had a dirt floor. When he was seven, his parents got a divorce, and it was, he relates, "the most painful thing that ever happened to me. When I was asked in court who I wanted to live with, I couldn't choose. I was hurting like crazy, but I found some relief in playing ball. I would throw a ball around for hours."

After a neighbor suggested that he start playing ball for a team, he really threw himself into the sport. "Baseball," he says, "was the biggest character-building influence of my youth. It taught me determination, perseverance, self-discipline, and patience. With these qualities, you are going to succeed at whatever you do." At fourteen, Olmos fell in love with music, and he brought the same qualities to music that he had brought to baseball. Although he claims to have no talent for singing, he taught himself to sing and play the piano. With some friends, he started a band and began his career in show business. In 1965, while he was attending college during the day and playing music at night to support himself, he took a drama course and got hooked on acting.

To support himself and the family he was starting, Olmos quit the band and started a moving business. When he wasn't lifting furniture, he studied and practiced his acting craft with the same determination and perseverance that he did everything else. By living very modestly and always improving his abilities, he was able to survive until he got his big break in 1978. The key to his success can be seen in his view on life.

"In the neighborhood where I grew up, we were all poor. The only way to survive was through a constant struggle of trying to be better today than you were yesterday. So that's what I tried to do. First with baseball, then later with music and acting, and I'm still doing that. When I speak to kids who have ended up in jail, I tell them we are all given a choice in life. They are born poor, or crippled; they had one parent, no parents or foster parents. Well, you can use any of these excuses to keep your life from growing. Or you can say 'Okay, this is where I am, but I'm not going to let it stop me. Instead, I'm going to turn it around and make it be my strength.' You can choose to be happy and work at life, or you can choose to be miserable and give up on it. I chose to work at it, and it worked for me."

Comprehension Questions

1. What obstacles did Edward James Olmos have to overcome to become successful?

2. What four personal qualities does he believe enabled him to succeed? What does each mean?

3. Someone said that to be successful, *"You have to choose to do, not what is easy and fun, but what is difficult but necessary."*
   How self-disciplined are you? In the following areas, do you make the effort to do what is easy and fun or what is difficult but necessary?

   1. what you eat

   2. homework

   3. class work

   4. exercise

   5. family relationships

4. In your own words, explain the significance of the title.

Succeeding:
OVERCOMING THE ODDS

"

I try to use words…

for human kind.

Never to create

anger but to reduce

anger, not to

separate people

but to bring people

together.

"

NEVER FORGET

ELIE WIESEL

I
N 1986, ELIE WIESEL was awarded the world's most prestigious honor, *The Nobel Peace Prize*. In giving him the award, the committee said, "He is a spiritual leader and guide in this age marked by violence, repression and racism." The walk to the stage to receive this award, however, represented a long and tortuous trip through life—a journey that no one would ever take voluntarily.

Born in Romania, Elie's first sixteen years were quite unremarkable. Elie was verbally and physically abused by the town bullies because of his religion, as other Jews were at that time in Romania. He was generally able to avoid going to town, though, and he lived pretty much in his own world. He described himself as a dreamer but very religious. "I was trained that the wasting of time was the worst sin, for time was meant to be devoted to the study of the Talmud, to the Torah, to prayer."

Then, early in 1944, his life turned into one of horror. He, his family, and all the other Jews in his town were arrested by the Nazis. Jammed into cattle cars, they were all transported to the Auschwitz concentration camp in Poland. His mother and younger sister died in the gas chamber. He did not learn that his two older sisters had survived Auschwitz until after the war's end. In the face of the advancing Russian army, the Germans sent Elie and his father to the Buchenwald concentration camp in Germany. At Buchenwald, as in Auschwitz, they lived every day with unimaginable horrors. Fed barely enough to stay alive, people died every day from starvation and disease. Those who didn't die in this manner were frequently shot or clubbed to death by the guards. Forced to work every day as slave laborers, any sick or injured person who fell was executed on the spot. Under these conditions, Elie's father fell ill and died.

Elie, however, survived all the horrors, and when he was seventeen, the camp was liberated by the American army. Not wishing to return to his old home, but unable to go to Palestine, Elie was put on a train with 400 other orphans. At the French border, the train was stopped. The children were asked if they wished to become French citizens. Elie did not understand the question, so he did not answer. As a result, he became a person without a country, but much later, he became a citizen of the U.S.A.

He gradually learned French and enrolled in school. After graduating, he worked at a series of newspaper jobs in France and the United States. Wiesel had a burning ambition to write of what he saw in the concentration camps. He believed that he survived when so many others died so he might bear witness to the horrors of the Holocaust. He made a promise to himself, though, that he would write nothing of his experience for ten years. "I didn't want to use the wrong words. I was afraid that words might betray it. I waited."

In 1956, he published his first book, *Night*. It is the story of a fifteen-year-old boy who feels guilty because he survived the horrors of the concentration camps while so many others died. Since that first book, Wiesel has gone on to publish almost two dozen more. As a teacher and writer in the United States, he says, "I try to use words...for human kind. Never to create anger but to reduce anger, not to separate people but to bring people together."

Comprehension Questions

1. What was Elie Wiesel's motivation for most of what he accomplished in life?

2. After being released from the camp, why do you suppose that the seventeen-year-old boy chose not to return to his home?

3. Another concentration camp survivor, Bruno Bettleheim, also wrote of his experiences. He observed that the difference between living and dying was sometimes nothing more than attitude. Those who were determined to survive, survived. While others, crushed by the violence and horror all around them, gave up the will to live. Write of an experience that you know of, where a person's attitude made all the difference.

4. In your own words, explain the significance of the title.

Succeeding:
OVERCOMING THE ODDS

"There were barriers still, it is true, but barriers that could in time be swept away."

A MUTE GENIUS

HELEN KELLER

AS A SYMBOL of one who overcame handicaps, no one is better known than Helen Keller. Her journey from ignorance, while locked in a deaf, blind, and mute world, to knowledge is a remarkable one. Because it is so amazing, plays, movies, and stories have been written about it, but her life needs a retelling.

Helen Keller was born normally. If scarlet fever had not struck her when she was nineteen months old, she probably would have grown up, grown old, and died with few people ever hearing about her. When she recovered from the fever, however, she was unable to see or hear.

At an age when children are beginning to speak to make their needs known, Helen couldn't utter a word. She had the vocal chords, but because she couldn't hear words, she couldn't reproduce words in speech. In her autobiography, *The Story Of My Life*, Helen tells of her frustrations at this time. "Sometimes I stood between two persons who were conversing and touched their lips. I could not understand and was vexed. I moved my lips and gesticulated frantically without result. This made me so angry at times that I kicked and screamed until I was exhausted."

As Helen got older, she could not help but get more frustrated and angrier. As a result, she became less responsive to her parents and more willful. She recalls, "I knew my own mind well enough and always had my own way, even if I had to fight tooth and nail for it." Her parents, more concerned than ever at their daughter's wild behavior, took her to Dr. Alexander Graham Bell. At his suggestion, they wrote to the *Perkins Institute*, a school for the handicapped. They asked if Perkins knew of a teacher who might work with Helen.

The *Perkins Institute* responded by sending Anne Sullivan to them. Sullivan, only twenty years old, was nearly blind herself. She had gotten an eye disease in the orphanage in which she had grown up, but Sullivan had learned much from her own difficult life. She recognized that to reach Helen, it was going to take firmness and determination. There were difficult times ahead for both of them. Under Anne's supervision, Helen seemed to be more rebellious than ever. In turn, the teacher became more strict and resolute. Her parents, who had always given in to Helen's tantrums, were wondering if they did the right thing in hiring Miss Sullivan. One day faded into the next, while everyone looked for the day when a breakthrough might occur.

When the breakthrough came, it came in a rush. Helen herself described the incident: "We walked down the path to the well, attracted by the fragrance of the honeysuckle with which it was covered. Someone was drawing water and my teacher placed my hand under the spout. As the cool stream gushed over one hand, she spelled into the other the word 'water,' first slowly, then rapidly. I stood still, my whole attention fixed upon the motions of her fingers. Suddenly I felt a misty consciousness as of something forgotten—a thrill of returning thought; and somehow the mystery of language was revealed to me. I knew that the 'w-a-t-e-r' meant the wonderful cool something that was flowing over my hand. That living word awakened my soul, gave it light, hope, joy, set it free! There were barriers still, it is true, but barriers that could in time be swept away."

From that moment, Helen's life changed. She could not learn fast enough. First, she learned to express herself through writing out letters; then she learned to read Braille. When she was ten, Helen heard about a deaf and blind Norwegian girl who had been taught to speak. Helen immediately resolved that she would learn to speak, too. With Anne Sullivan, Helen went and enrolled at the Horace Mann School For The Deaf where she learned to speak French and German, as well as English. After finishing high school, Helen went to Radcliffe College, from which she graduated with honors. After graduating, Helen and Anne Sullivan spent the rest of their lives writing and lecturing in an effort to improve the lives of the handicapped.

Comprehension Questions

1.   What made learning to read especially difficult for Helen?

2.   Once she learned what "w-a-t-e-r" meant, why do you suppose she was so eager to learn?

3.   What made her think that she could learn to speak?

4.   During the 19th and early 20th centuries, most of the children afflicted as Helen had been, never learned to speak or read. What do you think made Helen successful while so many others weren't?

5.   In your own words, explain the significance of the title.

Succeeding:
OVERCOMING THE ODDS

> "...sometimes you have to be hard on yourself when you are young, so the rest of your life will be easy."

IMMIGRANT WRITER

HOWARD FAST

MOST STUDENTS WHO have heard of Howard Fast, know him as the author of the novel *April Morning*. But in his long career, Fast has been the author of more than eighty books and at the center of many controversies. Because he was an admitted communist, American publishers refused to print his books during the 1950s. Thus, in 1961, when he published *April Morning*, it was the start of a second career. It is his first career, however, in which we are interested.

Like many immigrants to this country in the early 1900s, the Fastou family had its named shortened by U.S. immigration officials. Although a hard worker when he could work, his father had a difficult time supporting his family. When Howard was eight, his mother died. That year, to help support the family, Howard got a job delivering newspapers. Howard said that they were so poor that he and his brother stole bread and milk that had been delivered to the porches of rich people. They did this, he said, to keep from starving to death.

As he got older, Fast took on a series of better-paying, part-time jobs. Convinced of the importance of an education, he enrolled at George Washington High School. During this period, he worked for a cigar maker, a hat maker, a butcher, a dress factory, and for the New York Public Library. Until he got the library job, Howard's schedule was particularly difficult. After long hours in the hat or dress factory, hungry and tired, he caught the train home. Once at home, he had another three or four hours of homework before he could go to sleep. This period of Howard's life illustrates the old principle: Sometimes you have to be hard on yourself when you are young, so the rest of your life will be easy.

While working at the library, he became an eager reader, and he dreamed of becoming a writer himself. After he graduated from high school, Fast won a scholarship to the National Academy of Design and attended the academy for one year; however, he dropped out after selling a short story to a science fiction magazine. The sale of this story proved to him that he could realize his dream of becoming a writer. "It was the only way of life I ever considered," he wrote in his autobiography. "That is all I ever really wanted to do." He did not settle down to the craft of writing immediately, however. First, he and a friend left home and traveled through the South. Unable to find a job, he had to call his father for the bus fare home in order to avoid the prospect of working on a chain gang.

Returning to New York, he settled down to study the craft of writing and to write himself. Fast wrote two novels, but neither of them were successful. He recalls, "Suddenly everything dried up and I stopped writing."

Eventually, he did begin to write again and he completed his third novel. Although the novel was published, it did not sell well. Rather than being discouraged, Fast was more determined than ever to earn a living by writing. Shortly after this, he had his first big success when his short story, "*The Children*," was published. The story was based on his traumatic memory of the Halloween lynching of a black teenager by a gang of whites. The gang had earlier taunted Fast because of his Jewishness.

With this story as a launching pad, Howard Fast went on to become one of American's best selling novelists. Faith in himself, determination, and a willingness "to study his craft" paid off.

Comprehension Questions

1. What does the expression "sometimes you have to be hard on yourself when you are young, so the rest of your life will be easy" mean? How does it apply to Howard Fast?

2. What obstacles did Howard Fast have to overcome?

3. What qualities did he have that enabled him to reach his dream?

4. In your own words, explain the significance of the title.

Succeeding:
OVERCOMING THE ODDS

"I started to pay

attention to

the world instead

of taking it

for granted."

A SILENT WORLD

I. KING JORDAN

UNTIL HE WAS twenty-one, I. King Jordan's life was rather unremarkable. As a student, Jordan took little interest in school; he rarely opened a book or did his homework. Although he enjoyed taking typing and stenography classes so he could joke with the girls, he never went to the library or wrote a research paper. He spent many of his after-school hours jumping on his trampoline. He graduated from high school with a "C" average and was voted the "class clown" in his high school yearbook.

Not having any goals in life after high school, he joined the U.S. Navy and was assigned duty at the Pentagon in Washington, DC; he enjoyed the nightlife in that city. Spending his evenings partying, he danced in the clubs until dawn. In 1964, however, his life took a dramatic turn. While riding his motorcycle down a street in Washington, he was hit by an oncoming automobile. The collision sent him flying over the hood of the car. He landed on the windshield and cracked his skull. Somebody took his pulse and thought he was dead. A priest was even called to perform the last rites.

With a broken jaw and a fractured skull, Jordan appeared to have little chance of regaining his physical capabilities. His chances for regaining his mental capability were so slim that the neurosurgeon in charge of his case advised the Jordan family to, "pray that he dies." Not long after this, however, he regained consciousness; however, he was not released from the hospital until fourteen months later. Although he had lost the ability to hear, in all other respects his recovery was complete.

This experience had a great effect on Jordan. He says, "You would think the accident would have narrowed my world, limited me. But it did the exact opposite. I started to pay attention to the world instead of taking it for granted." Equipped with his new attitude toward life, he enrolled at Gallaudet University. At Gallaudet, a college for deaf students, he spent nearly all of his time studying. Sometimes he arrived at the library as early as 5:00 in the morning. In addition to motivating Jordan to focus his energies, his "invisible disability" also presented him with many challenges. As a former member of the hearing world, he had absorbed some of its prejudices, such as the idea that a deaf person was somehow less whole than a hearing person.

He says, "For years I thought of myself as only a visitor to the silent world. The attitude made me a loner in college. I was no longer fully accepted by hearing people, and not knowing the customs of the deaf world, I was socially awkward around other deaf students. Feeling like an outsider, I thought of quitting school."

Jordan, however, did not leave school. After graduating from Gallaudet, he enrolled in a graduate program at the University of Tennessee and attained a near-perfect record. He explains, "It was hard work, but not because I was deaf. An advanced degree is hard on anyone. I just spent more time in the library than most students. I read up on the material that they had heard in class."

With his advanced degree, he returned to Gallaudet University as an assistant professor, and he quickly worked his way up. In 1986, he was appointed dean of the college of arts and science. Then, in December, 1987, the President of Gallaudet resigned to become vice-president of a furniture company. Most observers felt that of the three people being considered for the job, I. King Jordan would most likely get it. However, the board of directors at the university, none of whom were deaf, chose the one candidate who could hear for the job. The campus exploded in student protest. As a result of this protest, the other candidate withdrew, and Jordan became the first deaf president of the first university dedicated to the education of the deaf.

In his speech to the students, Jordan said, "[These events show] the right of every person to have unlimited goals and expectations. I challenge you to try to do anything under the sun. I challenge you to succeed." No one can say what Jordan's life would have been like if he had not had that accident. His stubborn refusal not to be limited by his handicap, however, makes him a source of inspiration for everyone.

Comprehension Questions

1. Jordan says that until his accident, he took the world for granted. From context, what do you suppose he meant by that?

2. What was his reaction to his handicap?

3. Judging from the speech quoted in the last paragraph, what does he seem to feel may be a problem for deaf people?

4. In your own words, explain the significance of the title.

Succeeding:
OVERCOMING THE ODDS

> "
> *I wanted something*
>
> *to do where there*
>
> *seemed to be a*
>
> *challenge and a*
>
> *big future.*
> "

STAY HERE!

J. WILLARD MARRIOTT

J. WILLARD MARRIOTT, the oldest of four boys, was born on a ranch near Ogden, Utah, in 1900. He recalls the difficulties in his life: "We learned about adversity the hard way. One of my earliest memories is when the whole family had become ill with typhoid fever. As the oldest boy, I started work tending the family's sheep. At fourteen, I took on the adult responsibility for buying and selling the family's sheep."

After he turned eighteen, he spent two years doing the missionary work that is required of all young Mormon men and then returned to the ranch. Along with most sheep ranchers of the time, his father had gone bankrupt because the price of sheep dropped from $14.00 to $3.00 in one week. Determined that he and his brother and sisters would have a college education, though, Marriott studied and worked for the next six years. After attending Weber State College for two years, he transferred to the University of Utah. During that time, his occupations included running a clothing store and teaching high school English. He also managed a bookstore and sold woolen underwear to California loggers. After obtaining his B.A. degree, Marriott began teaching at Weber State College. He also served as the college's treasurer and theater manager to earn extra money.

Still, Marriott was more ambitious. "I wanted something to do where there seemed to be a challenge and a big future." During that year, a stand that sold root beer opened in Salt Lake City. This special drink was made according to a formula newly invented by two Westerners named Allen and Wright. Impressed by its success, Marriott decided to purchase the A & W franchise for the Washington, D.C., area. He knew Washington was hot and humid in the summer. For this reason, he knew it would be "a great climate for ice-cold root beer." Leaving Utah with money he had saved and borrowed, Marriott opened his first business. His root beer stand was in one half of a bakery shop he rented in downtown Washington.

With the help of his new wife, Marriott ran the root beer stand all summer. They had great success. But as winter approached, sales started to fall. Not one to be easily discouraged, he replaced the big orange root beer barrel in the window with a barbecue machine. Installing some stools and tables, he opened up his first *Hot Shoppe*. That winter, Marriott waited on customers while his wife cooked chili, tamales, and barbecue-beef sandwiches. Marriott quickly expanded his operations by employing promotional tactics, such as giving out free root beer coupons on street corners. By 1932, he had seven *Hot Shoppes* in the Washington area. The restaurants had varied menus with quality food. They also provided good service in clean, family-style surroundings. These *Hot Shoppes* were some of the earliest drive-in facilities in the East.

While many luxury restaurants failed during the Depression of the 1930s, the growth of *Hot Shoppes, Inc.* advanced steadily. In 1937, Marriott established an airline catering division. This came about after he noticed plane passengers carrying food on board from a *Hot Shoppe* near the Washington airport. Probably the most difficult time for the restaurant chain, however, was during World War II. At this time, automobile travel was restricted and most people were not eating out; but after the war, his business again picked up. By the mid-1950s, Marriott decided to branch out into hotels. Banking on his company's experience in the food and service business, he felt confident the hotels would also become successful. In 1957, the first *Marriott Motor Hotel* opened in Washington D.C.

In today's climate, J. Willard Marriott, who had worked fifteen to eighteen hours a day, would probably be called a workaholic, but he wouldn't see it that way. He once said, "No person can get very far in this life on forty hours a week." If the proof of a statement is in its result, J. Willard Marriott certainly proved that hard work does have its rewards. By the time he retired as chief executive in 1972, the Marriott corporation owned hotels and restaurants all over the world, including the Roy Rogers and Big Boy food chains. The company was earning over 315 million dollars a year and projecting sales of over 700 million dollars a year for the next year.

Comprehension Questions

1. What one quality of Marriott's seems to stand out as the reason for his success?

2. Marriott once said, "Good ideas are a dime a dozen." What does the expression mean, and how does it apply to his life?

3. Do you agree or disagree with his statement, "No person can get very far in this life on forty hours a week"? State your reason.

4. In your own words, explain the significance of the title.

Succeeding:
OVERCOMING THE ODDS

> " *Nothing is more common in this world than a person with talent who has wasted it because of a poor attitude.* "

COMING IN FIRST

JACQUELINE JOYNER-KERSEE

JACKIE JOYNER-KERSEE has been blessed with a great talent. If she had not, she could never have set two world records in twenty-six days. If she did not have this great talent, she could not have won two gold medals in the 1988 Olympics. Nor would she have been selected as amateur sportswoman of the year for two years in a row. Today, she is referred to as one of the world's greatest athletes. Yet, as Calvin Coolidge once pointed out, "Nothing is more common in this world than a person with talent who has wasted it because of a poor attitude." One thing that Jackie Joyner-Kersee never had was a poor attitude.

Born Jacqueline Joyner in East St. Louis, Illinois, she was named after President Kennedy's wife, Jacqueline. Her grandmother insisted on this name and predicted, "Someday this girl will be the first lady of something." Because her parents were teenagers themselves when Jacqueline was born, life was tough for the family. Both parents worked hard, but life in East St. Louis was difficult and dangerous. At the age of eleven, Jackie saw a man murdered right in front of her house. The house itself was no bargain. In the winter, the house had so little insulation that the water pipes froze. To take a bath in the winter, water frequently had to be heated on the kitchen stove. On really cold nights, the whole family slept in the kitchen since it was the only room with heat in it. Food, too, was sometimes scarce. Jackie remembers times that the family "ate mayonnaise sandwiches because there was no other food in the house."

At the age of nine, Jacqueline ran in her first race. She came in last. As she began to practice, she felt that she was improving. Sure enough, in the next few meets she won second places and first places. By the time she was twelve, she was leaping seventeen feet in the long jump. This feat inspired her older brother Al to begin competing in track and field events. He, too, would go on to be a gold medal Olympic athlete.

In the classroom, Jackie Joyner got the same satisfaction from her scholastic achievements that she got from her athletic prowess. In the fifth grade, the teacher explained how to do long division, but Jackie did not understand. She went home that night and spent hours working it out by herself. Eventually she got to sit at the front of the class. Less pleasing to Jackie was her mother's prohibition against dating before she was eighteen. At first angry and hurt, she finally accepted it. Without the distractions of dating, she threw herself even more fervently into athletic and scholastic achievement.

Jackie Joyner first took up an extremely difficult sport, the five-event pentathlon. A coach informed her that the quickest way to the Olympics was to master a variety of events. Blossoming quickly, she won the first of four consecutive National Junior Pentathlon Championships when she was fourteen. While attending Lincoln High School, she became known as the finest athlete in the state of Illinois. She set a state record by jumping twenty feet, seven and a half inches in the long jump in her junior year. She also starred on the Lincoln basketball team, and her team beat its opponents by an average of 52.8 points a game. She graduated in the top ten percent of her class, and she was recruited for both basketball and the pentathlon by the University of California at Los Angeles. Choosing the basketball scholarship, she enrolled at UCLA.

Midway through her freshman year, her mother died suddenly. From her grief, she said, "came a clearer sense of reality." She had always set goals and had been a striver. Now, however, she felt that she had inherited some of her mother's determination. With this thought in mind, she rededicated herself to succeeding.

While at UCLA, she was discovered by assistant track coach, Bob Kersee, who later became her husband. Maintaining a B average in her academic studies and starring in basketball was hard, and Jackie let her track skills slip, which upset Kersee. He said, "I saw this talent walking around that everyone was blind to."

Kersee went to the athletic director at UCLA and threatened to quit unless he was allowed to coach Jackie Joyner. His ultimatum met, he then went to Miss Joyner. He added up her personal best performances in the seven-event heptathlon. Her total score showed that without any special training, she was only 400 points behind America's champion heptathlete, Jane Frederick. Her sprinting ability in particular made her almost unbeatable in the 200-meter dash. Kersee knew her "raw speed was the best, but everyone could beat her in the hurdles." Bob Kersee persisted, and by 1982, he could see that she would be the world record holder.

In 1983, Jackie Joyner and her brother Al were selected to represent the United States at the track and field world championships held in Helsinki,

Finland. Because of an injury, however, she could not compete. She went on to win a silver medal in the 1984 Olympics and two gold medals in the 1988 Olympics. She had arrived. She had set her goals and reached them. In 1989 she returned to East St. Louis to raise money so the Mayor Brown Community Center could be reopened. In a speech to an audience of teenagers, she emphasized the importance of dreams and persistence:

"I remember where I came from and I keep that in mind. If the young females see the environment where I grew up and see my dreams and goals come true, they will realize their dreams and goals might also come true."

Comprehension Questions

1. Having gotten pregnant as a teenager, her mother did not want Jackie to fall into the same trap. But she also saw dating as a distraction from a young person's main job in life. In what way might dating distract someone from his or her goal?

2. If a fairy godmother promised that you would be successful by age thirty-five if you did not date or start dating until you were eighteen, how successful would you have to be before you went along with this?

3. In regard to Calvin Coolidge's statement, do you know of anyone with talent who is wasting or has wasted it because of a poor attitude? What was the talent, and what was the poor attitude?

4. What is your greatest talent? What would you like to achieve or accomplish with this talent?

5. In your own words, explain the significance of the title.

Succeeding:
OVERCOMING THE ODDS

"

If you reach for the

sky and tell the kids

what you are

reaching for, a lot

of them will reach

along with you.

"

A PRINCIPAL
WITH PRINCIPLES

JOE FERNANDEZ

FIFTY YEARS AGO, if someone had told Joe Fernandez he would one day be the number-one-man in the country's largest school system, he would have laughed. And he would have laughed a lot. At the time, Joe was a skinny teenager living in an apartment building on 126th Street in New York City. His former teachers would have agreed. Joe was less than a model student.

"My day consisted of getting up in the morning and saying good-bye to my parents as I told them I was going off to school. Instead, I would get on the subway and get off at Columbus Circle. There I would meet up with a group of guys and girls and we all walked down to 42nd Street. We didn't even bother to check into school." Today, Joe Fernandez is New York City's Chancellor of Public Schools and is in charge of nearly 1,000 schools and one million students.

Before becoming the head of New York's Public Schools, Joe had a rocky start. He grew up in poverty, the child of Puerto Rican immigrants. At sixteen, he dropped out of school and joined a gang called The Riffs. He has a scar on the right side of his nose that came from a Pepsi-Cola sign swung by an opponent during a turf fight. On the streets, he saw friends die of drug overdoses. He saw another friend stabbed to death in a bar. At seventeen, he decided he needed to escape the neighborhood or become a statistic, so he joined the Air Force.

He trained as a radio technician and managed to earn his high school equivalency diploma. Upon completing his training, he was sent to Japan and Korea. Joe got married in 1956 after his discharge from the service. Using his military benefits, he studied mathematics at Columbia University, but when a doctor told Joe that his sickly son needed a warmer climate, he packed his family in their station wagon and headed for Miami.

Joe worked as a postman and a milkman while finishing his undergraduate studies at the University of Miami, and he landed his first teaching job in 1963 at the Coral Park High School. Within one year, Joe had been promoted to chairperson of the math department. Joe's students said he made calculus and trigonometry come to life.

A friend from that time says, "Joe was always doing extra work and always looking for a way to better himself." During this time, Joe worked as a union steward, tutored students at home, and earned his master's degree. In 1971, Joe became an assistant high school principal in Miami. By 1987, Joe was appointed the head of the Miami Public School system and had earned a doctorate degree in education.

This former dropout had changed his life. Now his goal was to change the lives of the students in his schools. For this reason, one month after taking over the Miami schools, Joe made a surprise visit to an elementary school. The grass was uncut and the bathrooms were filthy. Joe transferred that principal immediately. Later, another principal was seen mowing his school's lawn on a Sunday afternoon.

Joe also started Saturday morning classes and opened specialized schools. These schools focused on the arts, computers, broadcasting, and other professional fields. Classrooms were set up in buildings donated by an insurance company, a community college, and the Miami Airport. In addition to simply improving the physical, Joe installed pride in the Miami School District.

In January, 1990, Joe became head of the New York's Public School System. The former gang member and dropout had returned to his old neighborhood with a goal. "Five years from now, I want the New York school system to be one of the best in the country." When asked if he could do it, Joe replied, "If you reach for the sky and tell the kids what you are reaching for, a lot of them will reach along with you."

Comprehension Questions

1. Like Danny Aiello, Joe Fernandez joined the armed services to escape from his environment. With the services being more difficult to get into, particularly for dropouts, what escape does a young person have today?

2. After quitting high school and joining the Air Force, Joe Fernandez got his G.E.D., a college degree, and two advanced degrees. What do you suppose happened to suddenly make him see the value of an education?

3. What sacrifices must Joe Fernandez have made to achieve success?

4. In your own words, explain the significance of the title.

Succeeding:
OVERCOMING THE ODDS

> "
> *It all began,*
>
> *however, with a*
>
> *mother's fierce*
>
> *determination.*
>
> *Add to this,*
>
> *a boy's burning*
>
> *ambition…*
> "

$500 TO $1,000,000

JOHN JOHNSON

JOHN JOHNSON is one of the richest African American men in The U.S. As a child, however, he was one of the poorest. This is the story of how this dirt-poor farm boy became the founder and owner of a publishing empire, an empire that is today worth more than sixty million dollars. It is a rags-to-riches story in the best tradition of America.

When he was six, John Johnson's father was killed in an accident at the sawmill where he worked. His mother, a fiercely independent woman, married again. But there was no question that her attention was still concentrated on young John. John graduated from eighth grade, but there was no money to send him to high school. Determined to keep him in school at any cost, his mother made him go back and repeat eighth grade. When he was fifteen, she made a momentous decision. Deciding that more opportunities existed for them in Chicago, she and John moved from Arkansas. The stepfather, at first reluctant to move, joined them later. For eighteen months, the family lived on welfare. Finally, the stepfather got a job with the WPA, a federal job program.

Johnson remembers the shabby clothes he had to wear while growing up in Chicago: "The other kids used to laugh at me and make fun of my homemade clothes. I decided I would show them, and I did." He enrolled at DuSable High School and quickly became an honor student. It was here that he also got his first taste of publishing. He became editor of the school newspaper and yearbook. He says, "I got interested in journalism and decided this would be my life's work."

On the basis of his record at DuSable High School, Johnson was invited to speak at a banquet to honor outstanding Negro high school seniors. Harry Pace, then president of the Supreme Liberty Life Insurance Company, was the main speaker on the program. Impressed with Johnson, Pace took him into his company as an office boy and also made it possible for him to study part-time on a scholarship at the University of Chicago. After two years, Johnson became an assistant to Pace. With this promotion, Johnson quit classes at the University of Chicago. He then devoted himself full-time to his work at Supreme Life.

One of his jobs was to help publish the company newsletter, which contained company reports and insurance business information. It also included some general news and information about black celebrities, businessman, and their families. Johnson's job was to clip out articles that he found in newspapers; Pace then selected those articles he wished to reprint in the company newsletter. Johnson realized that these reprinted articles deserved a wider audience. It was in this way he began to think of publishing the *Negro Digest*.

Using his mother's furniture as security, Johnson borrowed $500 from a loan company. Working nights, he printed the first edition of the *Negro Digest* on the insurance company presses. Johnson then mailed out 20,000 letters to Supreme Life customers offering charter subscriptions to his new magazine. Three thousand people responded by taking a subscription at $2.00 each. Promoting his magazine by working sixteen hours a day, Johnson eventually increased the circulation to 150,000 customers.

Happy with the success of the *Negro Digest*, Johnson began planning a picture magazine, patterned after *Life* magazine. The idea was to cover news and personalities in a more entertaining way than was done in the digest. It would, in Johnson's words, "show both Negroes and white people that Negroes got married, had beauty contests, gave parties, ran successful businesses, and did all the other normal things in life." The first issue of *Ebony* went on the newsstands in November, 1945. It immediately sold out its press run of 25,000 copies.

At first, the big companies were reluctant to buy advertising space in a magazine aimed exclusively at the African American market. In 1946, the president of Zenith Electronics met with Johnson, and Johnson got a contract with him. After this, Chesterfield Cigarettes, and International Cellucotton signed advertising contracts with Johnson. Others followed, and *Ebony* became the first all-Black publication to carry a significant amount of advertising from large U.S. corporations.

Johnson Publishing went on to publish *JET*, a pocket size news weekly, and *TAN*, a woman's service magazine. Johnson, who began buying stock in the Supreme Life Insurance Company in 1955, became its principal stockholder. It all began, however, with a mother's fierce determination. Add to this, a boy's burning ambition, a $500 loan on living room furniture, and you have an incredible success story.

Comprehension Questions

1. Horatio Alger wrote many stories at the turn of the century about boys who started out with nothing but ended up as millionaires through hard work. Why do you suppose those stories were popular back then? Is this type of story still as popular?

2. In Johnson's story, as well as in many other stories, the desire "to show them" is a strong and positive motivating factor in life. To some extent, we probably all share this desire "to show them." What people do you have a desire to prove something to, and in what positive manner might you show them?

3. Johnson's life is a perfect example of being prepared for luck when it hits you, or, as some people put it, you make your own luck. What lucky breaks came his way and why?

4. In your own words, explain the significance of the title.

Succeeding:
OVERCOMING THE ODDS

> " I realize the
> challenge of life is to
> have the energy to
> continue exploring
> all the roads that
> have opened up and
> following them
> to the end. "

SMALL PACKAGE

LINDA HUNT

YOU MAY REMEMBER her as the tiny but tough principal in Arnold Schwartzenegger's "*Kindergarten Cop.*" However, it was for her role as a male Eurasian that she won her Oscar. The night Linda Hunt walked onto the stage in Los Angeles to accept the Oscar as Best Actress in a Supporting Role was a memorable one. The walk down the aisle to the stage, however, capped a remarkable journey by a truly remarkable person.

When she was six months old, her parents suspected a problem in her development, and a doctor in New York confirmed their fears. There was a problem. He suspected that baby Linda had such a severe birth defect that she would eventually have to be hospitalized for the rest of her life. He had labeled her condition, incorrectly, as cretinism, which is a condition that results in the stoppage of mental and physical development in early childhood.

Fortunately, her parents had the time, resources, and knowledge to work with her. And work with her they did. By the time she started school, she had improved greatly. Still, she was much different in size and appearance than her classmates. As a result, as children sometimes do, they treated her cruelly because she was different. Hunt recalls, "I was totally alienated almost from the first day. I had a bad experience with a teacher and she made me feel stupid. I felt bad that I didn't fit in. What I had going for me, however, were my parents. They never stopped encouraging me in every way they could."

When she expressed an interest in acting, her parents hired someone to coach her. Then, in 1969, they sent her to Goodman School of Drama in Chicago. It was at this time the doctors discovered that she suffered from a form of dwarfism. This condition is a result of the pituitary gland not releasing enough growth hormones. Over the next ten years Linda sought medical help to correct the problem, but her efforts had little success.

The staff at the Goodman School, because she weighed only eighty pounds and stood four feet nine inches, encouraged Linda to go into directing rather than acting. Because of her appearance, they apparently felt that she would have a hard time getting acting jobs. Her dream, however, was to act, so when she finished school, she went to New York. After three years, feeling discouraged and defeated, she returned home. She was ready to give up her dream, "but my acting coach reminded me again about the importance of acting in my life. I had lost myself for a while and that awareness gave me back to myself. Soon I was sending out resumes and reading for parts."

Slowly, with small parts, her career inched forward. Then came "*The Year of Living Dangerously*" and her Academy Award. Since then, there have been many more stage and screen parts. Hunt says, "I'm working more than I thought I'd be, but not as much as I'd like. I'm still feeling frustrations about myself and my career. There are moments of total despair and darkness. Thankfully, I believe there are always answers. I realize the challenge of life is to have the energy to continue exploring all the roads that have opened up and following them to the end.

"When I was a child, I always thought I would be on the outside. That is, I would always be outside the group, while everyone in the group was on the inside having fun. Now I realize that at times in their lives everyone feels on the outside. I find that I love people and they love me. I feel very lucky."

Comprehension Questions

1. What was Linda Hunt's dream, and what obstacles did she have to overcome?

2. She had a great deal of help and encouragement from her family, but what personal qualities enabled her to finally achieve her dream?

3. Given her physical appearance and early school experiences, it is understandable why she felt "on the outside." However, why does just about everyone feel like an outsider at some time or other?

4. In your own words, explain the significance of the title.

Succeeding:
OVERCOMING THE ODDS

> "
> *Every time I went*
> *to a new school, I*
> *wanted to be at the*
> *top of the class.*
> *I wanted to be*
> *number one.*
> "

WORKING HARD WORKS

LUPE VASQUEZ

FOR LUPE VASQUEZ, the battle to be number one started when she was two years old, when her mother decided to move the family from Mexico to Arizona.

Her mother, who had only a sixth-grade education, wanted a better life for Lupe and her brothers and sisters and thought that it could be found in Arizona. Lupe's mother started work there as a live-in maid. However, she was treated very badly and paid very little. Lupe's family then went to work in the fields as migrant workers. Because migrant workers must follow the crops being harvested, the workers and their families are constantly on the move. As a result, children often go to several schools within one year.

Adjusting to a new school, new teachers, and classmates is hard. When you have to do this three or four times a year, it is especially difficult. It can make getting an education almost impossible. Some students give up in frustration. Lupe's mother, however, made sure Lupe studied. "My mother," said Lupe, "always told me to do well in school. 'If you don't want to work in the fields or clean houses, study hard. You deserve better.'"

Lupe remembers her mother leaving for work every day at five or six in the morning and not getting home until late afternoon. Even after working these hours and coming home bone-tired, her mother always found time to work with Lupe. She taught Lupe her ABC's, numbers, and colors in Spanish. When Lupe was six, she enrolled in first grade, but she could not speak English. With no English language classes being offered, Lupe had to learn English by listening to her classmates.

English was not the only thing Lupe learned from her classmates; she learned how to compete academically. "Every time I went to a new school, I wanted to be at the top of the class. I wanted to be number one. I guess I needed to compete against the other kids to show them who I was," Lupe said.

109

Because of the migrant worker's need to move frequently, Lupe had many opportunities to show her classmates who she was. During junior high school, her family moved seven times. A more severe hardship, though, was to follow. In her junior year of high school, Lupe's family was evicted. Having no relatives to turn to for help, the family had to live on the streets. After a few terrifying days and nights, the family was finally taken in by a shelter for the homeless. It was in such a shelter that Lupe spent her last two years of high school. While caring for the four younger children, she studied and did her homework in the television room.

Lupe had decided early in her life to go to college, and she never lost sight of that goal. "I thought that with a college education, I'd be able to get a good job and help my mother out," Lupe said simply. "Originally I decided to apply for an Army ROTC scholarship to pay for college, but some friends suggested that I also try for other kinds of financial aid, too."

At a friend's insistence, Lupe applied to Stanford University in California. To her surprise, the University awarded her $10,000 in financial aid. She also received awards from the federal government and private scholarships toward her college education. In September, 1991, Lupe began her freshman year at Stanford, planning to become an environmental engineer, so she could make a difference for her family and her world. Her studying and perseverance had paid off. She was now able to attend one of the most prestigious universities in the country. Lupe, however, is not waiting for a college diploma before improving her world. Every week, Lupe goes to a housing project where a young Hispanic grade-school student awaits Lupe's lessons.

"I don't think anyone should have had to go through what I went through. It isn't right for kids to be exposed to that kind of situation. There's so much potential in them, but they don't show it because of the obstacles they face."

Lupe said she had an internal drive that made her want to get out of poverty. Her teachers, who have said she was very bright, would not call her a genius. Instead, they say: "She got where she is today by good, old-fashioned, hard work."

Comprehension Questions

1. Most people, like Lupe, are not geniuses. Unlike Lupe, however, most of us do not live up to our potential. What is the difference between Lupe and most of us?

2. If you had children, how would you encourage them to work up to their abilities and not just slide along?

3. What obstacles did Lupe have to overcome?

4. Why do you suppose Lupe felt a need to show people "who she was" and be an outstanding academic student?

5. In your own words, explain the significance of the title.

Succeeding:
OVERCOMING THE ODDS

> "
> *...she had to get*
>
> *an education, for*
>
> *only with money or*
>
> *knowledge would*
>
> *she have the power*
>
> *to get things done.*
> "

NEVER TOO LATE

MARIE BALTER

MARIE BALTER'S mother was an alcoholic and her father deserted the family when she was an infant. As a result, baby Marie wound up in a foster home when she was four. When she was six, she was adopted by a middle-aged couple. This was unfortunate because some couples should never have children, and this was one of those couples. The rules in the house were strict, and punishment was harsh. Worse than that, the couple was never able to give love or receive it from this vulnerable child. When she tried to crawl into their laps, they would just push her away.

The breaking point came when Marie was fourteen. One of their many rules was that Marie had to be in the house when the streetlights came on. One evening as she was walking home, the streetlights came on. Running home, she pounded on the locked door and begged to be let in. Her father opened the door, looked at her and said, "Go away." Slamming the door in her face, he said, "You don't live here any more."

Through a social agency, Marie was sent to a boarding school in Boston. She did well there until her senior year. Overcome by a feeling of great depression, she could do nothing. She felt, "I am alone. I am abandoned by everyone. Nobody cares about me."

At the hospital, doctors felt they could not help Marie, so they transferred her to Danvers State Hospital. At the State Hospital, they mistakenly decided she was suffering from schizophrenia. As she describes it in her autobiography, *Sing No Sad Songs*, her life at the hospital was year after year of drug-filled horror. In one of her semi-lucid moments, she remembered making her way to the hospital's chapel. There she made this solemn promise to God:

> *Dear God, if you help me leave this hospital, I will remember everything I've been through and use it for those I leave behind.*

Shortly after promising this, a medical crisis developed. In a reaction to the drugs they had been giving her, Marie went into a toxic coma. When she came out of it, the doctors withdrew most of the medicines they had been giving her. Gradually, Marie got a little better. After eighteen years of hell in the hospital, she was on the road to recovery.

A year after getting out of the hospital, Marie had married and gotten a steady job. The vow she had made in the hospital chapel stayed with her, however. She knew if she was really going to help the mentally ill, she had to get an education, for only with money or knowledge would she have the power to get things done.

Friends pointed out that she hadn't been in a classroom in twenty years. Also, she was thirty-seven years old, and still had attacks of anxiety. True, her new medicine helped her get over the attacks, but would the pressure of school throw her back into the hospital? It was a question she had to consider. With the encouragement of her husband, however, she enrolled in a community college and, after earning a two-year degree, enrolled in Salem State College, where she began to work towards a Bachelor's Degree in psychology.

No sooner had she begun the program, than her husband was rushed to the hospital. On New Year's Day, her husband died. Once again, Marie felt abandoned. Feelings from her childhood swept over her. Remembering her vow, however, she threw herself into her studies. Upon graduation, Marie returned to Danvers State Hospital. This time, she was there as a fully accredited social worker. But to accomplish all she wanted to, Marie realized she needed an advanced degree and applied to the University of Texas. She was rejected, though, because she had once been a mental patient. Well-intentioned friends told her to forget it. "Get on with your life," they said. However, she had also applied to Harvard University. To everyone's surprise but Marie's, she was accepted, and in 1982, she graduated from Harvard with a Master's Degree.

Marie eventually became a director at Danvers State Hospital, and she now has the power to change things to help the mentally ill. Perhaps, though, more than anything she can do in the future, it is what she has done in her own life that will affect people most. This child, abandoned and rejected, overcame the traumas of her childhood and made a success of her life. Her achievement is far greater than the accomplishment of any millionaire.

Comprehension Questions

1. What goal did Marie set for herself, and what obstacles did she have to overcome to achieve it?

2. With what prejudice does someone like Marie have to deal?

3. Why was getting an advanced college degree so important to Marie?

4. In your own words, explain the significance of the title.

Succeeding:
OVERCOMING THE ODDS

"

Not only did she

survive the pain of

her early life, but

she went on to use it

to build her life.

"

WRITING'S HER STYLE

MAYA ANGELOU

MAYA ANGELOU is a woman of many talents. She is an actress, singer, dancer, songwriter, teacher, editor, and writer. Today, most people recognize her as a poet and author of her autobiography, *I Know Why the Caged Bird Sings,* but life had not always been bright for her. She escaped a life of poverty, emotional trauma, and drug addiction. She says she still wrestles with the demons from her past.

When she was three, her parents divorced. Her mother, a beautiful woman, did not wish to live the life of a single mother with two young babies to look after. For this reason, she sent Maya and her brother to her parents' home in Arkansas. Although Maya speaks of feeling rejected by her mother, she also recalls this period of her life as one "of a lot of love and so much humor."

At the age of seven, she and her brother returned to St. Louis to live with her mother. What followed was a nightmare for this sensitive seven year old. Maya was raped by her mother's boyfriend. At first, Maya told no one. When she finally did tell her brother, he told some of their uncles. When the man was found the next day kicked to death, Maya felt responsible for his death. She felt that in speaking his name, she had caused his death. Fearing the power of speech, Maya became a voluntary mute. For the next five years, she spoke not a word to anyone. Throughout this period, she read a great deal and developed a strong inner life. It was her reading of poetry aloud that finally led her back to speech. She began by reciting poems aloud to her brother. Then she recited poems to others. Finally, she again began to speak. However, the dark period of her life was not yet behind her.

At sixteen, the day after she graduated from high school, she gave birth to a son. During the next several years, she was involved in the seamy side of San Francisco nightlife. Drugs and other illicit activities became part of her life. Determined to turn her life around, though, she enrolled in evening courses in dance and drama. Then, on a full scholarship, she moved to New York and studied dance. After leaving the dance school, she became a nightclub singer and dancer. From there, she moved to the stage and went on a touring company production of Porgy and Bess. Her professional life jumped ahead in leaps and bounds after this.

During this period, Angelou became involved in the Civil Rights Movement. She worked as a coordinator for Dr. Martin Luther King's Southern Christian Leadership Conference. Following that, she spent a year in Africa as a teacher and administrator at the School of Music and Drama at the University of Ghana. She wrote, "Africa to me is more than a glamorous fact. It is a historical truth. No man can know where he is going unless he knows exactly where he has been and exactly how he arrived at his present place."

Back in the United States, Angelou, who felt that the black woman had never been portrayed faithfully in films, wrote the screenplay *Georgia, Georgia*. Later, she would also write the screenplay and music for *I Know Why the Caged Bird Sings*. She added another first to her career when she went on to direct the film. Of the black female she has said, "She has nursed a nation of strangers, and has remained compassionate. This to me is survival. She is strong. I am very surprised with her." The reader can say no less about Maya Angelou. Not only did she survive the pain of her early life, but she went on to use it to build her life. She is a remarkable woman and an inspiration to all who go up against the odds, and not only survive, but win.

Comprehension Questions

1. Maya Angelou is obviously a very talented person. Yet, she came very close to never realizing the talent she had. At what point do you suppose her life could have gone down the drain?

2. What saved Maya Angelou from going the same way thousands of other young people have gone?

3. When she says that she "still wrestles with the demons from her past," what message of hope is there for all people who had traumatic childhoods?

4. In your own words, explain the significance of the title.

Succeeding:
OVERCOMING THE ODDS

> "
> *At each step along*
>
> *the way, he had to*
>
> *struggle against*
>
> *overwhelming odds*
>
> *to succeed, but*
>
> *succeed he did.*
> "

THE MAYOR'S
HARD ROAD

RICHARD HATCHER

ONE OF THE FIRST black mayors of a major northern city in the United States was Richard Hatcher of Gary, Indiana. His story is a classic success story. At each step along the way, he had to struggle against overwhelming odds to succeed, but succeed he did.

During the Depression, Richard's father lost his job at the Pullman Company. Shortly after Richard was born, the family moved to the worst slum in Michigan City, "The Patch." For the mother, father, and seven children, life, which had never been easy, became almost impossible. To get fuel for the two coal stoves that heated the house, Richard remembers walking along the railroad tracks picking up chunks of coal that had fallen off the trains. He recalls, "In the winter, there were never enough covers. I remember how unhappy we would be when my father would tell us that we had to let the fire go down at night because otherwise there wouldn't be enough coal the next day."

Food, too, was not easy to come by. The little money his father could earn by working odd jobs or salvaging things put meat on the table, at the most, once a week. More often, their supper was just biscuits and syrup. Some days, he remembers, he could not go to school because he had no shoes to wear. Through all the bad times, however, he remembers how the love of his family sustained and inspired him. "One of my earliest recollections is of my father encouraging me to make something of myself. I remember seeing the well-dressed kids in school and hoping that someday I could look like them."

In *Up From The Ghetto*, a book that contains short biographies of fourteen successful black people, Richard related the following to the authors: "I recall how determined I was to go to college. This was a pretty ridiculous hope under the circumstances. I guess, though, that young people are more optimistic than anyone else." When he was a junior in high school, his father got regular employment. As a result, they were able to move out of "The

Patch" to a better house. The night Richard graduated from high school, he told his father that he wanted to go to college. His father responded that there just was not the money to pay for it. "I told him that one way or another I was going to go on to school." Working that summer at the Pullman Company, Richard saved all his money. He added several hundred dollars that was collected for him by his church. With this, and by waiting on tables in the school's dining hall, Richard was able to get through his first year at Indiana University. To get through the next three years, he had to do the same.

After graduating from the University, he decided he wanted to go on to law school, and he enrolled in the law school at Valparaiso University. He worked an eight-hour shift in a hospital in the evening and went to class during the day.

Despite this difficult schedule, Richard graduated from law school with honors. Richard credits his success and the success of his brothers and sisters to the drive to succeed in the family, particularly his father's desire to see his children become somebody. Because of this intense desire, he says that his father was willing to make many sacrifices.

After a short and successful career in private law practice, Richard joined the county prosecutor's office. He quickly moved on to the post of deputy prosecutor. Then, although it meant taking a pay cut, he resigned his position and ran for the City Council in Gary. Four years later, he decided to run for the office of mayor. It would be, he knew, a rough and tumble, uphill battle. When in his life, though, wasn't it a battle? Fighting against entrenched politicians and dishonest officials, he waged a vigorous and hard campaign. When the votes were counted, he was Mr. Mayor.

Comprehension Questions

1. Mayor Hatcher, like many of the people we profiled, was raised in poverty. He and the others we have written about were unusual in that they were able to become financial successes. But the majority of people in these circumstances aren't able to do so. What, do you suppose, makes it difficult for people to break this poverty cycle?

2. How do people like Richard Hatcher, Clarence Thomas, and Anna Langford break out of the poverty cycle?

3. If, in fifteen years you had a child who did not want to go to school "because it is so boring," what would you say to your child?

4. In your own words, explain the significance of the title.

Succeeding:
OVERCOMING THE ODDS

> " *She remembers*
> *repeating to herself,*
> *'I will be a singer. I*
> *will succeed.'* "

NOTHING COMPARES 2 HER

SINÉAD O'CONNOR

SINÉAD O'CONNOR is known as an international singing star, but life wasn't always rosy for this young girl. Sinéad was born in Dublin, Ireland, the third of four children. When she was eight, her parents separated, and her troubles began. Her mother, perhaps because of the breakup of her marriage, was an unhappy woman.

Over the next five years that she lived with her mother, Sinéad was frequently beaten. She remembers lying on the floor and covering her face while her mother kicked her. She also recalls how she tried to deal with it. "I remember trying to tell people—getting on the school bus and telling the conductor, but no one wanted to hear. My way of reacting to all this was that I stole all the time and I skipped school. No one sat me down and said, 'What is wrong? Why are you doing this?' Even though everyone knew what was going on. The result was that I was made to feel I was a terrible person. The real problem was brushed under the carpet."

It was during this period that Sinéad stole things from stores and collected money for charities that did not exist. She says, "I was trying to make my mother happy by getting money for her. Between the ages of nine and thirteen, I must have been dragged to police stations about eight or nine times. I never got charged with anything, though, because I used to put on the waterworks. I would say, 'Oh, my mother will kill me.' I think I used to believe it myself. So I never actually got charged with anything."

When her mother felt she could no longer control young Sinéad, she shipped her off to live with her father and stepmother. Sinéad continued to steal, however; she even stole money from her father and stepmother. When she was caught stealing a pair of gold shoes from a store, it was too much. At the age of fourteen, she was sent by her parents to an institution for delinquent girls that was run by Dominican nuns.

Sinéad says, "I have never—and I probably will never—experience such panic and terror and agony over anything such as this. I caused my parents a lot of trouble, but I couldn't express myself any other way. Running riot was my way of dealing with things."

It was at this institution that Sinéad had her first experience with musical success. As it happened, the brother of one of her teachers was the drummer for a popular Irish band. Impressed by her singing voice, he asked her to work with his group. With this encouragement, she wrote "*Take My Hand,*" which the band performed. While the song did not become a national hit, its success did a great deal to encourage the unhappy teenager.

When she was released from the institution at age sixteen, her parents sent her to a boarding school 150 miles from Dublin. She and the school, however, did not get along. "Everyone from Dublin was considered real strange and especially me, because I had shaved hair and I wore strange clothes. It was a very closed community. It took a year and a half before anyone would speak to me, because they considered me too weird."

Desperately unhappy, Sinéad left the school to live on her own in Dublin. She knew that if she was to have any career in music, she had to be in Dublin. She remembers repeating to herself, "I will be a singer. I will succeed."

To support herself during this period, she played guitar and sang on street corners and in bars. At one point, she supported herself by singing telegrams while dressed in a French maid's uniform. Finally, she connected with a band that was playing the larger pubs in Dublin. There she was heard by two record producers. At the age of twenty, she recorded "*The Lion and The Cobra*"; and not long after this, she recorded her second album. This record contained her biggest hit to date, "*Nothing Compares 2 U.*"

While Sinéad may never completely recover from the trauma of her childhood, she was lucky she had her music to comfort her. She was fortunate, too, that she had the musical talent to accompany her determination. As a result, Sinéad came out a winner.

Comprehension Questions

1. Sinéad was fortunate she had musical talent. As a runaway, what kind of life might she have had in Dublin if she did not have the talent?

2. What advice would you give a friend who is thinking of running away?

3. What obstacles did Sinéad have to overcome?

4. In your own words, explain the significance of the title.

Succeeding:
OVERCOMING THE ODDS

> " I believe that
> I am not an
> extraordinary
> person. I am
> simply living up
> to my potential. "

THE PIZZA MAN

TOM MONAGHAN

TODAY, TOM MONAGHAN, the founder and owner of Domino's Pizza, is one of the richest men in America. But Tom started with nothing. In fact, some people would say that he started with less than nothing. After the death of their father, Tom's mother sent him and his brother to an orphanage. At the age of twelve, Tom left the orphanage and lived in a series of foster homes. Tom, however, had a strong belief in God and in himself; he also had a burning desire to make something of his life.

Tom doesn't brag about his accomplishments. If asked, however, he will tell how he achieved success:. "In four words, Faith, Desire, and Hard Work are what did it for me. I believe that I am not an extraordinary person. I am simply living up to my potential. I believe that everyone should do as much as he can, as well as he can, regardless of his job or station in life. I find it very hard to believe that anyone who wants to work can't get work of some kind. From the time I got out of the orphanage at twelve, until I got into the pizza business at twenty-three, I had forty jobs. I knew I was born to work. I never drew unemployment in my life."

Tom quickly admits that the job you can get may not be the job you want, but he says, "You have to start somewhere. I have college graduates, who, because they have a college degree, think they cannot take any job but a manager's position. Who in the world," he asked, "is going to hire a college graduate without any experience in the business as a manager? I believe that you take the job you can get at the time. Then you work your way up. The guy who sits around waiting for the 'right job' to come up, could sit doing nothing for a long time."

Another point Tom is emphatic about is honesty. He believes that you can't take short cuts or play the angles. "A friend of mine from the orphanage had a bright future ahead of him in one of America's best corporations. He had worked his way up in the purchasing office, but he had taken some money under the table from a supplier. His company found out about it and fired him. He has not been able to make a go of it since then. Those things always catch up with you."

While Tom believes in planning and working toward a goal, he got started in the pizza business by accident. Withdrawing from college after one semester, Tom and his brother bought a pizza parlor in Ypsilanti, Michigan, in 1960. Because the pizza parlor was not making it, they had to come up with only a $75.00 down payment. In his autobiography, *Pizza Tiger*, he says, "At that point, I would have opened just about any business I could, as long as it only required a little or no down payment."

Although he says he was cheated many times in those years by people he trusted, he didn't lose his faith in people or in his own vision. Working eighteen hours a day, seven days a week, he and his brother made a success of that first store. Despite suggestions from others that they expand their menu, they concentrated on pizza and soda.

After buying out his brother, who wanted to move on to other things, Tom's vision became even clearer. He planned to own a chain of pizza shops that delivered tasty, hot pizzas at a reasonable cost in a reliable, speedy manner. By 1973, just thirteen years after he opened that first shop, his company had seventy-six stores in thirteen states. After that, the company just took off. There are now more than 5,000 stores, and they are in just about every state in the union.

Although he has a vintage automobile collection worth thirty million dollars and some expensive real estate, Tom maintains he still lives a simple life. Tom and his wife still work in the company. His children, who get no allowance, have only the money they earn for spending money. While he may have "the bucks," he and his family will not become part of the "idle rich."

Comprehension Questions

1. In what way was Tom "tough on himself so life would later be easy on him"?

2. What things did Tom have to sacrifice in those years? In your opinion, were the sacrifices he made worth it?

3. What sacrifices would you be prepared to make to be a success?

4. Why does he say you can't take shortcuts?

5. In your own words, explain the significance of the title.

Succeeding:
OVERCOMING THE ODDS

He made me

believe that I could

make something of

myself, but that it

was completely

up to me.

TOP COP

WILLIAM CELESTER

In the 1990's, William Celester was the Police Commissioner for the city of Newark, NJ, but he wasn't always on the right side of the bars. In fact, at the age of sixteen he was sent to jail for six months for non-support of his child. By the time he got out of jail, he was even more bitter and cynical than before he went in. "I hated the system," he says. "I was convinced it was racist and that it would never give someone like me a chance."

Up to this point, William Celester's story is not all that different from the story of any other poor, black, inner-city kid. When William was four, his father abandoned the family. In ninth grade, he dropped out of high school and joined a gang, the Marseille Dukes. "In an area like that," he says, "being in a gang gives you a sense of belonging. There were about six rival gangs and each thought they were the *"baddest."* But in those days, we didn't fight over drugs, we had turf wars. While we usually didn't fight with guns, our president was shot to death in a street fight. For myself, I didn't think that I'd live to see twenty. At the time, I couldn't have cared less. You can see I wasn't one of those kids who grew up dreaming of becoming a cop."

After getting out of jail, William returned to the corner and his old life. Then a break came for William that marked a turning point in his life. A community youth worker told William that she could get him a good paying job if he were willing to work hard. Soon, William was making good money as a sandblaster at the navel shipyard, a big step forward for him because all of his earlier jobs had been low-paying, dead-end jobs.

The next break for William came from a former state senator, Royal Bolling. Bolling thought that William had a lot of promise and encouraged him to think and plan for the future. William says, "Royal became a father-figure and mentor for me. He made me believe that I could make something of myself, but that it was completely up to me. More than that though, he convinced me that hating only holds you back and eats you up. In the end, you waste a lot of time and energy in hating, and you're the one most hurt by it."

133

In 1966, Bolling encouraged William to take the examination to become a Boston policeman. At the time, there were only thirty-five Black police officers on the entire city police force, and when William was growing up, there were even fewer. As a result, the police officer was never thought of as friend to William and his gang. "That," pointed out Bolling, "was the point. Things don't change by themselves, people change things by taking the first step."

While he recognized the truth of this, William was still reluctant to take the exam. He was sure that the police department would never accept him. Again Bolling pointed out that he was defeating himself before he even tried. "Take the first step; apply and see what happens." William did, and in August 1968, he joined the Boston police force as a patrolman and resolved to make something of himself.

His first test came early in his career. Assigned to a civil rights demonstration, some of the blacks at the demonstration called him an "Uncle Tom." They said he was a traitor by being a Boston policeman, which hurt him very much, and he began to question his decision. Upset, he went to his mentor, Royal Bolling. He told Bolling, "I want to make things better for myself and my people, but it doesn't seem that I'm accomplishing that. I feel like quitting the force."

Bolling looked him squarely in the eye and said, "If everyone quit at the first sign of trouble, or the first time they felt discouraged, nothing would ever be accomplished. In that case, we would never be able to change things. Do right, work hard, and hang in there. In the end, you will be amazed at what you accomplish."

William did stick it out, and a year later he got his high school diploma through the G.E.D. program. He then enrolled in college and earned a four-year Bachelor's Degree. Three years later, he earned a Master's Degree. It wasn't easy working full time, going to school, and raising a family, but William had a plan and a goal that helped him to "hang in" when things got tough. His goal was now attainable. He had the experience, and he had the academic credentials. After working his way up through the ranks in the Boston Police department to the rank of Deputy Superintendent, he was offered and accepted the job of top cop in Newark, NJ.

Comprehension Questions

1. How did Commissioner Celester use the system to make something of his life?

2. What obstacles did he have to overcome?

3. How do bitterness and anger become obstacles to success?

4. What qualities did William have to have if he were to reach his goal?

5. In your own words, explain the significance of the title.

Succeeding:
OVERCOMING THE ODDS

"
He never gave
up…he continued
to have a positive
attitude, and he
always crossed the
finish line.
"

DRIVEN

BEN COMEN

I N 2005, A SPECIAL kind of eighteen-year old senior attended Hanna High School in Anderson, South Carolina; Ben Comen believed he had been put on this Earth to set an example. He devoted a significant amount of his free time to volunteer work, helping to build wheelchair ramps for the Easter Seals, helping the elderly in assisted-living homes, and working with Habitat for Humanity to build homes for the poor. This extraordinary kid, himself afflicted with cerebral palsy, was even featured in *Sports Illustrated*, but not because of his volunteer work.

According to the magazine, Ben is "the slowest cross-country runner in America." Despite his dedication and hard work, the disease, which reduces the body's ability to control its muscles and motion, slowed Ben down and prevented him from enjoying life in the same ways most other people do. Cerebral palsy, fortunately, did not affect his intellect; in fact, Ben maintained very good grades. But he needed to run to feel better about himself.

Running with cerebral palsy was very difficult, and made winning nearly impossible, but Ben did not mind losing, nor did he care. Ben wanted only to be part of a team. For years, his parents tried to find a team for their son to play on, but no one would let him play. Coaches would let Ben be in charge of water, or minor equipment, but he was never allowed to participate. Finally, Ben's mom got in touch with the cross-country coach at Hanna High. Ben was welcomed to the team when he was in the eighth grade, he ran with it for five years, and most importantly, he was treated as an equal. His teammates welcomed him immediately, and became his closest friends. Ben's perseverance was admirable. He never gave up—even though running 3.1 miles took him nearly an hour, he continued to have a positive attitude, and he always crossed the finish line.

Attending one of Hanna High's cross-country meets was a touching experience. Ben's cerebral palsy caused him to fall numerous times throughout the race. Falling down would not have been so bad if Ben's brain had only been capable of sending warning messages to his hands so he could catch himself. However, his brain worked very slowly in communicating with his muscles; when Ben tumbled, he fell hard, which left him bruised and bleeding by the end of every race. Fortunately, Ben's team was very supportive. After the runners on his team crossed the finish line, they turned around to finish the race with Ben—their fellow teammate and friend. Everyone cheered him on and gave him encouragement until the end.

For most people, falling down frequently, losing constantly, and having to be bandaged up after every race would be very discouraging, but that's exactly what kept Ben going. He wanted to beat his own personal records and prove to himself that he was capable of being a good athlete. Ben proved that no one has to be perfect to succeed. Regardless of Ben's track record, he was extremely successful. Being on his high school cross-country team introduced Ben to new people, allowed him to belong to a team, and helped him to achieve his own personal goals.

Through his adversity, Ben achieved many goals; ultimately, he set a marvelous example for kids and adults—reach for your dreams, set goals, work hard, and never give up. Anyone can be a winner!

Comprehension Questions

1. What was the name of Ben Comen's high school, and where was it located?

2. What did Ben believe he was been put on this Earth to do?

3. What selfless acts did Ben do in his spare time?

4. Why was Ben Comen featured in Sports Illustrated?

5. What made Ben so slow? Why?

6. Did Ben care if he won a race? Why or why not?

7. What did Ben's teammates do at every race?

8. What has Ben taught you by reading this article?

9. In your own words, explain the significance of the title.

Succeeding:
OVERCOMING THE ODDS

"

…it taught him

extremely

important life

lessons such as the

value of not giving

up, the importance

of following dreams,

and a special

appreciation for

life itself.

"

LIVE STRONG

LANCE ARMSTRONG

Some people spend their adolescence deliberating and debating about what direction to take in life. There are those who long to learn medicine, practice law, or become concert pianists. For others, the future is not a question because they know, from a very young age, what they were born to do.

Lance Armstrong was born to be a professional athlete. At 13, Armstrong won the Iron Kids Triathlon (swimming a mile, cycling thirty miles, and running nearly seven miles), which started his career in the right direction. This win strengthened Armstrong's desire to become a professional athlete by the time he was 16, and it was also around this age that Armstrong began to like bike racing more than the other two sports. By his senior year of high school, he was good enough to train with the U.S. Olympic cycling team.

Through his determination and natural talent, Armstrong became the U.S. National Amateur Champion. The next year, he competed in the 1992 Barcelona Olympics cycling race, but didn't win a medal. He also participated in his first professional race, the Classico San Sebastian, that year. Unfortunately, he came in last; however, the loss made Armstrong more determined to press on, and he strengthened and improved his cycling skills. In 1993, the 22-year-old won the U.S. PRO Championship, raced in the Tour de France, became the youngest road racing World Champion, and won the $1,000,000 Thrift Drug Triple Crown. Also in this year, Armstrong's cycling team became the first U.S. team to be ranked in the top five in the world.

In 1996 he was ranked as the number one cyclist in the world. Lance Armstrong was becoming a household name, especially in Europe, where cycling is second in popularity only to soccer, but disaster lurked around the corner.

Later in 1996, Armstrong received news that would change his life and career forever. During a routine ride, he experienced a pain so strong that he was unable to continue. In October of that same year, he was diagnosed with advanced testicular cancer, which had also spread to his lungs and brain, seriously threatening both his career and his life. He underwent two complex operations—one to remove the cancerous testicle, and the other for the rest of the cancer. In addition to the extensive surgeries, Armstrong began chemotherapy. This nightmare of frightening events did not deter the cyclist; he remained positive. Three months following his diagnosis, he formed a non-profit organization, the Lance Armstrong Foundation, to help improve cancer awareness and research. (You have probably seen his trademark yellow "Live Strong" bracelets; as of 2005, over 47 million of them have been sold.) Armstrong's chemotherapy was a success and, amazingly, he was back on his bike within five months.

Armstrong absolutely refused to allow the life-threatening cancer to change his dreams; the disease, the treatment, and the fight against cancer gave him further inspiration and determination to continue toward his goals. In 1998, Armstrong returned to professional cycling. While he participated in the Paris-Nice race, the weather turned so treacherous that it was extremely difficult for him to continue. Tired and frustrated, Armstrong pulled over, vowed to quit cycling for good, and returned to his home in Texas. Shortly after he moved home, though, a group of close friends took him on a trip to North Carolina to help him learn "to love the bike again." Their plan was a success, and Lance Armstrong bounced back.

With high spirits, and with his positive attitude renewed, Armstrong began his world record Tour de France winning streak. Racing in 1999, he won by over seven minutes; in 2000, he won the race by six minutes. But, one day as he was training, he was hit by a car. The accident fractured a vertebra, but, miraculously, he still made it to the Olympics and came home with a Bronze medal. In the years 2001-2005, Armstrong added five more consecutive Tour de France victories to the two he already had. No one had ever won more than five of the most famous bike races in a row. Lance became one of the world's most recognized athletes and, in the process, also became a millionaire.

Armstrong said that his cancer was "a special wake-up call," and it taught him extremely important life lessons such as the value of not giving up, the importance of following dreams, and a special appreciation for life itself. Lance Armstrong has made a name for himself, not only as an athlete, but also as a survivor. The world has honored him for his struggles and his accomplishments.

Comprehension Questions

1.   What was Lance Armstrong's first victory? How old was he?

2.   What is the most popular sport in Europe?

3.   What was Armstrong's "special wake-up call"?

4.   Three months following his diagnosis what did Armstrong do? Why?

5.   What did Armstrong do five months after being diagnosed?

6.   What made Armstrong want to ride in a bike race again?

7.   What was Armstrong's major accomplishment?

8.   In your own words, explain the significance of the title.

Succeeding:
OVERCOMING THE ODDS

> "
> *...even as he found*
>
> *himself close to*
>
> *death, he knew he*
>
> *could survive.*
> "

SPLIT DECISION

A R O N   R A L S T O N

LIFE IS FULL of risks, but that does not stop people from sky diving, hang gliding, mountain climbing, or white-water rafting. Adventurers have found an infinite number of ways to test life's limits. However, with thrills also comes the risk of danger. There is always a chance that tragedy or even death is lurking around the corner.

The challenge of risk-versus-reward came true for Aron Ralston, a 27 year-old avid hiker and an experienced rock climber, who has climbed fifty-nine of the tallest peaks in Colorado, forty-five of which he scaled alone. One Saturday morning, April 26, 2003, Ralston decided to spend his day hiking through canyons, unaware that this one-day trip would turn into a five-day-long fight for life.

Bluejohn Canyon, Utah, was Ralston's destination. The beautiful scenery and the many canyons to explore made him anxious to get started. Ralston did not even realize, however, that he was about to make a huge mistake, one that could cost him his life. Before exploring solo, Ralston should have informed park officials of his intended whereabouts for that day—just in case—but he didn't. Ralston was equipped with all he thought he'd need for a day hike: climbing gear, less than one quart of water, a small first aid kit, a multi-use tool, a video recorder, and two burritos in his backpack.

Canyoneering is a relatively new sport, in which hikers and rock climbers descend by ropes (rappel) into the depths of canyons, exploring and discovering nature's marvels from the inside. Ralston practiced this sport that Saturday by rappelling into a three-foot wide area. He encountered an enormous boulder, and as he slid off, intending to continue through the canyon, the huge rock shifted, pinning his arm. With his arm trapped in the clutches of a boulder weighing approximately 1,000 pounds, Aron began his fight. He, fortunately, did not panic, which could have killed him. Instead, his initial thought was to use his knife to try to chip away the rock and free his arm; diligently, he worked for ten hours, but he made absolutely no progress toward freedom.

Sunday and Monday, he tried different methods to free himself and rationed his tiny food and water supply. It was Tuesday when Ralston's supplies finally ran out. Desperate, he decided that the only way he was going to survive was to amputate his own arm. The arm was already completely numb, so he knew that the pain would be bearable. Ralston did not have many items to choose from, so he had to use his cycling shorts as a tourniquet. Then, Aron attempted to saw off his arm using his cheap, dull pocketknife. After a few hours cutting through the skin and finally reaching the bone, he knew that the only way he could cut through the bone was with a bone saw—the dull blade would never do the job.

Aron doubted that he could do this, and decided to wait until some other hiker wandered nearby, but no one did. When he realized that his attempts for freedom were lost, Ralston began to doubt that he would ever survive. He even etched his name, date of birth, and his expected date of death into the side of the boulder. By Wednesday, Ralston was forced to drink his own urine to stay hydrated, and then he recorded a message for his parents on the video recorder. Thursday, his fifth day trapped in the Utah canyon, Aron Ralston felt that in order to survive, there was only one way to do it.

With his remaining strength, he broke the bones in his right arm and began sawing relentlessly through the remaining tissue, skin, and muscles, which took approximately one hour.

Finally free, but very weak, Ralston created a sling from his equipment, took his rock-climbing gear, and exited the canyon. He rappelled down a cliff nearly 70 feet high using his one remaining arm and hiked five miles in the heat until he met a family that was camping in the park. The mother and son went for help, while the father stayed with Ralston, giving him food, water, and first aid.

Ralston was taken to the nearest hospital and, amazingly, made a full recovery. His will to live proved to be strength enough to make it through this tragic accident. Park officials said that it would have been nearly impossible to find Ralston because of the location of the canyon—it is in an area of the park that is rarely explored. In addition, it took thirteen men to retrieve the remains of Ralston's arm from behind the monstrous boulder. Doctors fitted Ralston with a modern, completely functional prosthetic arm that he believes will be superior to his flesh, blood, and bone original.

Aron Ralston never let nature, or tragedy, defeat him. The days spent in that canyon were dismal, but even as he found himself close to death, he knew he could survive. Ralston knew he had more of his life to live, and he is determined to do more traveling, more canyoneering, and more exploring whenever and wherever he can, despite only having one arm.

Comprehension Questions

1. What experience had Aron Ralston had before his excursion through Bluejohn Canyon?

2. How many of the fifty-nine peaks did Ralston scale solo?

3. What was Ralston's huge mistake the day he decided to explore in Bluejohn Canyon, Utah?

4. What is canyoneering?

5. How wide was the area where Ralston became lodged behind the boulder?

6. How did Ralston finally free his arm from the crag?

7. Would you have done the same if you were in Ralston's situation? Why or why not?

8. In your own words, explain the significance of the title.

Motivational Quotes

"You may have a fresh start any moment you choose, for this thing that we call "failure" is not the falling down, but the staying down." - **Mary Pickford**

"People with goals succeed because they know where they are going...It's as simple as that." - **Earl Nightingale**

"The first step to becoming is to will it." - **Mother Teresa**

"The indispensable first step to getting the things you want out of life is this: decide what you want." - **Ben Stein**

"Our attitudes control our lives. Attitudes are a secret power working 24 hours a day, for good or bad. It is of paramount importance that we know how to harness and control this great force." - **Tom Blandi**

"Don't spend your precious time asking 'Why isn't the world a better place?' It will only be time wasted. The question to ask is 'How can I make it better?' To that there is an answer." - **Leo F. Buscaglia**

"Confidence doesn't come out of nowhere. It's a result of something...hours and days and weeks and years of constant work and dedication." - **Roger Staubach**

"Be Prepared!" - **Boy Scout Motto**

"If you don't like something, change it. If you can't change it, change your attitude. Don't complain." - **Maya Angelou**

"If you wish to know the road up the mountain, ask the man who goes back and forth on it." - **Zenrin**

"I am not discouraged, because every wrong attempt discarded is another step forward." - **Thomas A. Edison**

"We've got to have a dream if we are going to make a dream come true."
- **Denis E. Waitley**

"Experience is not what happens to a man; it is what a man does with what happens to him." - **Aldous Huxley**

"Success is a journey, not a destination." - **Ben Sweetland**

"Be happy in the moment, that's enough. Each moment is all we need, not more."
                                                                    - **Mother Teresa**

"If not you, then who? If not now, then when?" - **Hillel**

"The men who try to do something and fail are infinitely better than those who try to do nothing and succeed." - **Lloyd Jones**

"Chance favors the prepared mind." - **Louis Pasteur**

"Your chances of success in any undertaking can always be measured by your belief in yourself." - **Robert Collier**

"If you're never scared or embarrassed or hurt, it means you never take any chances." - **Julia Sorel**

"The one without dreams is the one without wings." - **Muhammad Ali**

"One can have no smaller or greater mastery than mastery of oneself."
                                                                    - **Leonardo da Vinci**

"If we all worked on the assumption that what is accepted as true is really true, there would be little hope for advance." - **Orville Wright**

"Great hopes make everything great possible." - **Benjamin Franklin**

"Concentrate all your thoughts upon the work at hand. The sun's rays do not burn until brought to a focus." - **Alexander Graham Bell**

"You may get skinned knees and elbows, but it's worth it if you score a spectacular goal." - **Mia Hamm**

Insightful and Reader-Friendly, Yet Affordable

Prestwick House Literary Touchstone Editions–
The Editions By Which All Others May Be Judged

Every Prestwick House Literary Touchstone Edition™ is enhanced with Reading Pointers for Sharper Insight to improve comprehension and provide insights that will help students recognize key themes, symbols, and plot complexities. In addition, each title includes a Glossary of the more difficult words and concepts.

For the Shakespeare titles, along with the Reading Pointers and Glossary, we include margin notes and eleven strategies to understanding the language of Shakespeare.

Special Introductory Educator's Discount – At Least 50% Off

New titles are constantly being added; call or visit our website for current listing.

		Retail Price	Intro. Discount
200102	**Red Badge of Courage, The**	$3.99	$1.99
200163	**Romeo and Juliet**	$3.99	$1.99
200074	**Heart of Darkness**	$3.99	$1.99
200079	**Narrative of the Life of Frederick Douglass**	$3.99	$1.99
200125	**Macbeth**	$3.99	$1.99
200053	**Adventures of Huckleberry Finn, The**	$4.99	$2.49
200081	**Midsummer Night's Dream, A**	$3.99	$1.99
200179	**Christmas Carol, A**	$3.99	$1.99
200150	**Call of the Wild, The**	$3.99	$1.99
200190	**Dr. Jekyll and Mr. Hyde**	$3.99	$1.99
200141	**Awakening, The**	$3.99	$1.99
200147	**Importance of Being Earnest, The**	$3.99	$1.99
200166	**Ethan Frome**	$3.99	$1.99
200146	**Julius Caesar**	$3.99	$1.99
200095	**Othello**	$3.99	$1.99
200091	**Hamlet**	$3.99	$1.99
200231	**Taming of the Shrew, The**	$3.99	$1.99
200133	**Metamorphosis, The**	$3.99	$1.99